RESTORED

Discover Freedom
from
Love Addictions, Guilt, and Shame

As culture continues to celebrate and affirm various sexual identities and the church struggles to respond with truth and grace, the need for biblical insight becomes all the more critical. In her book *Restored*, Leslie Anderson shares firsthand the struggle and victory that come with surrendering one's same-sex attraction to the Lord and learning to trust in His goodness as He heals and transforms. I highly recommend this book, not only for women but for everyone looking for hope and freedom in Christ.

> – Jason Thompson,
> Executive Director, Portland Fellowship

Restored is a book that any woman who has or is currently experiencing same-sex attraction would find useful and encouraging. Leslie Anderson has lived the life and writes from her experiences and her many years of understanding since leaving a lesbian life. She writes of the roots and influences that may take a woman into a lesbian relationship. She notes that the dream of finding true fulfillment with another woman may not turn out to be as hoped.

The book shows that to choose Jesus is to choose life itself. By learning God's ways and purposes, a woman can grow into a deeper relationship with God that has healing, and victory over the many challenges in life. Anderson uncovers the kinds of battles many Christians encounter. She gives insight into deception and the luring toward human idolatry that can be experienced. Then she gives helpful instruction on how to deal with these things.

She speaks of the many benefits there are to remaining in Christ. Staying the course leads to such promise not just for this life but also the next. The final chapter leaves the reader with a feeling of exuberance and victory. It reminds of the promise of God for a fruitful and good life here, then a glorious life forever. I would recommend any woman who struggles with same-sex attraction read this book. I would recommend women who are not same-sex-attracted but who find themselves trapped in false promises of romantic liaisons outside of God's plan to also read this book as they too may relate to the wisdom written in *Restored*.

> – Dr. Shirley Baskett,
> Past Director of Renew Ministries, Australia/Pacific,
> Author of *The Woman Who Outran the Devil*

In reading *Restored*, I appreciate the tools Leslie Anderson has put together for those desiring to overcome same-sex attraction from her own life experiences. In her book, she weaves relatable stories in with scripture and how the Lord met her as she continued in her journey, which gives hope to the reader. I very much recommend this book for anyone wanting to find freedom from the lifestyle by surrendering to and following Jesus.

> – KathyGrace Duncan,
> Women and Transgender Ministry Leader, Portland Fellowship

Restored is a vulnerable writing of a woman's journey out of homosexuality.

To follow along with what happened in her life, as well as reading of the people, the books, and scriptures that helped her along the way would benefit anyone who is going through the same struggles.

I hope this book finds its way into many hands to bring hope not only to individuals seeking help, but also for those believing for more in the lives of their loved ones.

> – Carmen Vaught,
> Leader Liaison, CHANGEDmovement.com

Restored

Discover Freedom
from
Love Addictions, Guilt, and Shame

Leslie Anderson

I will seek what was lost and bring back what was driven away, bind up the broken and strengthen what was sick.
Ezekiel 34:16

Restored: Discover Freedom from Love Addictions, Guilt, and Shame

Copyright © 2024 Leslie Anderson

Published by Reify Press, Aurora, Oregon.

Scripture quotations are from the NKJV unless otherwise noted.

Scripture taken from the New King James Version®. Copyright © 1982 by Thomas Nelson. Used by permission. All rights reserved.

Scripture quotations taken from the Amplified® Bible (AMP), Copyright © 2015 by The Lockman Foundation. Used by permission. lockman.org

Scripture quotations marked NLT are taken from the Holy Bible, New Living Translation, copyright © 1996, 2004, 2015 by Tyndale House Foundation. Used by permission of Tyndale House Publishers, Inc., Carol Stream, Illinois 60188. All rights reserved.

For privacy's sake, all names have been changed.

ISBN 978-1-949638-14-1

Dedication

To all those addicted to love

May those addicted—to anything at all—find hope for freedom in this book and in God's word, as I did.

As you learn what your Good Shepherd will do for you, you will be able to say with King Hezekiah:

You will restore me and make me live . . . You have lovingly delivered my soul from the pit of corruption.

– Isaiah 38:16, 17

Contents

Part I – Wandering Far from Home

One	Living My Truth	3
Two	It's about Love, Isn't It?	9
Three	Coming Home	14

Part II – Journey of Restoration

Four	Healing Your Heart	19
Five	Feeding You Well	25
Six	Support If You Fall	31
Seven	Dealing with Opposition	39
Eight	Evading Deception, Traps, and Detours	47

Part III – Doing Your Part

Nine	Walk Closely with Jesus	57
Ten	Following Jesus	65
Eleven	Wholehearted Living	73

Part IV – Looking Ahead

Twelve	Entering the Promised Land	83
Appendix A	Steps to Becoming a Follower of Jesus	94

Introduction

What makes people risk everything and put it all on the line? Sometimes, it is drugs or alcohol, a cause they believe in, and for some, it is love. For me, it was love—or what I thought was love.

I was a pastor's daughter gone prodigal. I left a ten-year heterosexual marriage, alienated my friends and family, and risked losing custody of my preschool children, all for a same-sex relationship.

The first few years felt free and liberating, and we were energized by fighting for custody of my children. (Part of that energy was outrage that we even had to engage in that battle.)

We had beautiful times together, but relationship difficulties eclipsed them after a while. I could hardly endure the pain when we fought, but the love also felt strong, and I didn't think I could live without it. I often wanted to leave but didn't have the strength to do it. It took me a while to realize that I was addicted to love.

In addition to our relationship problems, I saw things over time in the gay community that disturbed me, and I began to question how I lived. And then, occasionally, I felt Jesus gently tug at my heart.

Finally, after thirteen years, Jesus found me and gave me the strength to leave that relationship. In those early years of following Him, I longed to know if anyone had left life as a gay person and stayed with it. Were they able to have a happy life? Was Jesus enough to fill the void of not having a partner, and did they live faithfully for Him? The bigger question was whether I could do it and stick to it.

After thirty-five years of walking with Jesus, I can testify that anyone struggling with same-sex attractions and issues such as pain from childhood traumas, various addictions, or guilt or shame can find lasting freedom.

I want you to know that it is worth it to follow Jesus, and you can trust Him to set you free. Life is better with Jesus, and there is a way out of living in gay relationships. Jesus has given me a wonderful life with healing friendships, exciting adventures, restoration of family relationships, and the peace and joy of walking with Him.

Most of the material in this book is from the Bible, my testimony, those of others, and resources such as books and podcasts. This book will let you know the following:

- How to walk closely with Jesus
- How to understand the roots of feelings
- How to avoid a "close call"
- How to face opposition
- How to cope with difficulties
- How to find resources and extra help.

(If you are unsure you belong to Jesus, please refer to Appendix A, which explains how to make sure.)

There is a beautiful passage in Ezekiel in which God is described as a Shepherd looking for His sheep: *"I will seek what was lost and bring back what was driven away, bind up the broken and strengthen what was sick"* (Ezek. 34:16). Scholars tell us that this passage refers to God bringing Israel back from captivity. Some say it applies to all of us in the millennium.[1]

The Bible says we are like *"sheep going astray"* (1 Peter 2:25). Jesus is described as the Good Shepherd who gave His life for His sheep (John 10:15). He gave His life for us, looks for us, brings us home, and nourishes us back to health. I was lost and broken when He found me, and I'm so glad He came searching for me and brought me home.

I love the story of the woman at the well who told people about her encounter with Jesus. The Bible tells us the people listened to her testimony until they met Jesus and then listened to Him (John 4:39–42). I hope that is what you will do.

If you have never met Him, let me introduce you to Jesus, your Good Shepherd. He won't let you down if you follow Him, and you can trust Him to heal you in a way that's just for you. Your Good Shepherd knows where you are and is calling your name. He wants to set you free and bring you home.

He will feed His flock like a shepherd;
He will gather the lambs with His arm,
And carry them in His bosom,
And gently lead those who
are with young.

– Isaiah 40:11

Part I

Wandering Far from Home

1
Living My Truth

I screamed as loud as I could. There they were—a group of Christians holding signs covered with scriptures. My partner and I were waiting to attend a gay men's chorus performance when we noticed grim and unsmiling faces in the crowd around us. They were trying to stop the hiring of a gay teacher in a nearby city.

I yelled something ugly. The gay teachers I knew were people of integrity and skilled in their work. How could these Christians be so unfair? This was my first, but not my last, experience of people screaming in protest.

My anger was fueled by the custody battle I was fighting for my two preschool children. My ex-husband tried to cut me out of their lives and get full custody because of my gay relationship. I was a good mother, and I knew it was wrong to lose my kids because I loved another woman. It was the 1970s, so there was a good chance he could win in the courts during those years, and my former Christian friends were on his side.

I tossed and turned many nights, worrying about losing my children. The up-and-down battle lasted several years. The lines were drawn. I was in anguish. At the time, experts advised that divorce was the best thing we could do for our children if we were unhappy. I learned more about that years later.

My partner and I were able to remain positive during the custody battle with the help of our friends from our gay church and others. They provided sympathetic ears as we went through various levels of estrangement from family and friends.

My partner had a good sense of humor, and we would laugh a lot, get together with our friends, and talk about how terrible all those Christians were. This bothered me at times because, growing up, I knew sweet Christians who loved Jesus, and I did, too.

My mother told me about Jesus through the "Wordless Book" when I was four years old. I prayed to receive Him and felt His presence from childhood through early adulthood.

In the years before my divorce, I quit reading the Bible and praying. My husband and I attended church but were busy working and moved often, so we didn't have a Christian support group. By the time we went to counseling for our marital issues, I had met her and so was dishonest about this relationship with him and with the counselor.

My Christian friends had various reactions when I left my husband. One lady traveled from another state to see me and wrote scripture verses in lipstick on my bathroom mirror.

Another couple invited my husband and me to a church service with them and walked us to the front altar at the end of the service, hoping I would change my mind. I went along, but my heart was closed. I was no longer listening to His voice.

My parents reacted more harshly than anyone else. My dad was a Bible school student and planning to become a pastor. I brought this lady I loved to their house to meet them, but they wouldn't let us in. My dad screamed at us from the backyard that we were from the devil. We sat in the car and cried.

When I left my husband, I told myself the Bible describes only a part of God. The Bible was no longer my rule for life. After all, He commanded us to love one another, and I felt a powerful love for this woman. I often pictured God looking down and being okay with two women who loved each other, like seeing two female horses nuzzling each other in a pasture.

My partner and I had a lot of good things going for us despite all the negativity we received from some people. We traveled worldwide and had a lovely home and good friends. We loved entertaining and even hosted a brunch for a star from the television show "M*A*S*H." We had fun most of the time.

It's interesting to read the testimonies of other people who have lived in gay relationships in the past but came to faith in Christ. They talk about some of the good times living as gay people.

Beckett Cook, who has a YouTube channel by that name, talks about his twenty years designing movie sets and socializing with movie stars.[1] Dr. Christopher Yuan was captivated by the drug scene and a busy social life when he lived as a gay man.[2] Dr. Rosaria Butterfield had a good life as a tenured women's studies professor teaching "queer theory."[3] Like me, they all enjoyed *"the passing pleasures of sin,"* as described in Hebrews 11:25. But then they reached a point where they met Jesus and made a U-turn.

Beginning to Question

The pastor's "wife" fell flat on her face, sobbing. We all sat in stunned silence. How could this women's retreat go so wrong? My partner and I were part of our urban gay church's women's group, and we were all gathered by a river in a secluded spot. A gay couple we admired led our church: a female pastor and her partner of eleven years.

Louise, our pastor, started the service by saying she and her assistant were now a couple. This was the first her partner heard of it, and she was overcome by emotion. But Louise ignored her former partner and led us all in communion. Then, she and her new partner went to the river and baptized one another.

"What kind of church is this?" I wondered. I knew "regular" churches had issues, but I had never experienced anything so horrible.

My partner and I had attended this church for many years. The sermons were all the same, talking about Jesus and how He would fight for oppressed people like us. We enjoyed being a part of it, but this put things in a different light.

On a day like this and other days, questions about my lifestyle began to enter my mind.

One terrifying time was when my eleven-year-old daughter was near the point of death from an unknown infection, and I began to wonder if God was angry at me. But my partner and my friends surrounded me in support, and someone gave me a gay theology book to read. The ideas in that book eased my questions for a while.

There was a young man during those years who would visit our church and preach. He was a dynamic speaker and assured us our lifestyle was okay with God. He would visit periodically as the years went by and, in later years, began talking about how much fun it was to "come out" in the leather scene. (The leather bars promote kinkier types of sex.) His countenance seemed darker each time he preached.

Some gay women friends with professional jobs told us they were into "S and M" (sado/masochism) and encouraged us to do the same. We also knew that the "man/boy love" group was quietly working for acceptance. (The term "M.A.P."—minor-attracted people—is now used to describe these types of groups.)

These things raised questions for me. "Where is the line?" I wondered. "What determines if something is moral?" I often thought of the Darwinian model, survival of the fittest, and realized the world would be harsh and confusing if it became our guide. But I kept my questions to myself because "political correctness" was common even then.

Death also haunted me. I would see dead bodies at funerals and wonder what happens after people die. I read books about near-death experiences and wondered if people had bad experiences after death. I didn't believe in hell, but I feared it might exist.

Maybe this describes you as well. You once had a close relationship with Jesus and have many happy memories of your years in the church, Bible studies, prayer, and walking with Him. But then, as time passed, "life happened," and you got too busy or moved and disconnected from your faith community. Maybe those same-sex attractions you once pushed down began to surface, and you invited all kinds of speculations into your head. Then, over time, you ended up in a same-sex relationship.

You may have found love and acceptance with a gay partner and with others in the gay community, and you may be enjoying some good things in life. Perhaps you have found a church that agrees with your viewpoint, and you feel like Jesus is on your side. You have seen much support but sometimes notice things that aren't so good.

You might be having fun in Egypt and receiving support from others. You may be living your "truth," but a part of you may have questions deep inside.

You probably try not to think about all this too much, but there are moments when the "noise" of your life is quiet, and you begin to wonder. Those moments only increase with time.

2

It's about Love, Isn't It?

But this deeply satisfying friendship became the road to my anguish because soon I discovered that the enormous space that had been opened for me could not be filled by the one who opened it. I became possessive, needy, and dependent, and when the friendship had to finally be interrupted, I fell apart. I felt abandoned, rejected and betrayed. Indeed, the extremes touched each other.

Henry Nouwen, The Inner Voice of Love

When you're in love with another woman, you often find that you're so similar to each other that it's easy to lose your identity in each other. You become each other in an unhelpful way. As I've sought freedom from lesbian relationships, I've realized that I don't want to lose who I am to who I am with. An essential part of me is lost when I give myself to another woman in a way I was never supposed to.

Anne Witton, blog entry, February 2023[1]

These quotes are good descriptions of my relationship and probably many lesbian relationships. I became obsessed with keeping it going and made a lot of personal compromises to do so. Her slightest look of displeasure would send me spinning. I would do anything to maintain the relationship.

When we had a conflict, I would feel devastated and begin researching to understand what was wrong. I would read books about boundaries because I knew I was giving in to my partner too much. It wasn't her fault, but I would do whatever it took to keep the relationship alive. When my partner was happy, I was happy; when she wasn't, I wasn't.

At one point in our relationship, we went to couples counseling. We did that for several months, which helped some, but not enough. I began to go to Al-Anon meetings on my own.

Al-Anon gave me a name for what ailed me: codependency. The twelve-step program was helpful and included "sought through prayer and meditation to improve our conscious contact with God."[2] I realized I hadn't quieted my heart to seek God for several years, and I began to see that I was putting my partner in God's place. I was serving her, and it was a form of worship.

I was losing my sense of self; even though I didn't realize it then, it was bondage. Beckett Cook described this type of bondage in his video, "Why Does God Care about Your Sex Life?"[3] He stated he never knew he was in bondage while living as an active gay man until later when he realized how much he was wounded "spiritually and emotionally."

Later, I learned that the fear of death is a type of bondage as the Bible describes in Hebrews 2:15: *"release those who through fear of death were all their lifetime subject to bondage."*

Little by little, my mind opened to making changes, but life was too stressful and busy to think much about change. I pushed these thoughts back when times were good, and when they were bad, I attended Al-Anon meetings.

The reality of all I had given up would nag at me when what I thought was love began to wear thin.

It seemed worth it until it didn't.

It felt like love until it didn't.

Gentle Whispers

As I walked downtown one day, a book on the street grabbed my attention. I picked it up and saw it was about Bible prophecy. It had a picture of a puzzle on the front cover with a few missing pieces. I read it in a day or two, not wanting to put it down. It described many things the Bible prophesied would happen to complete the puzzle just before the end of the world.

We studied these Bible prophecies when I was a child, and I learned what would happen in the "last days." There would be a one-world government and a one-world leader, and people would have to have a "mark" to buy and sell. We read in the Bible that wars, famines, and earthquakes would increase in frequency.

I could see many of the pieces of this puzzle coming together in the world around me, and I began to wonder if the Bible was true. How could the Bible predict these events with such accuracy?

The re-emergence of the state of Israel in 1948 was another thing that I often wondered about. How could that have happened unless it was by the hand of God?

I Need More . . .

Evidences of Christianity

➢ Alisa Childers podcast:

"An astrophysicist tells how science led him to Jesus" Interview with Hugh Ross.

– November 1, 2022

➢ Alisa Childers podcast:

"Do we have actual evidence for the resurrection of Jesus?"

Interview with Gary Haberman, who has done extensive research on this topic.

– August 14, 2022

The shroud of Turin captivated me. I read credible stories about the shroud bearing an electronic image of the face of Jesus. Was this evidence of the resurrection?

At times, I thought about the fact that the disciples of Jesus turned from fearful men to men willing to die for Him after His resurrection. Why would they do that unless they knew the resurrection was true? If the resurrection were true, then Christianity had to be true.

My life was also impacted by some believers I met over the years. One sweet neighbor lady invited us to the single's group at her church. I wondered if she had any idea how we were living. But she was so friendly and kind. I'm sure she never knew how much her sweet attitude affected me.

Two believers at work touched my heart when I overheard them discussing their faith. Even though they talked about problems they had in their lives, I could see the light in their countenances.

Another time, I saw a group of Christian women surround a hospital bed to pray for someone. Their faces seemed to glow with joy, and I envied them.

As I began putting everything together, I wondered if Christianity and the Bible were true. I would ask myself: "If the Bible is true, do I need to follow the Ten Commandments and its guidelines on sexuality?"

I knew I was guilty of breaking the first commandment to have no other gods before Him (Exod. 20:3). Idolatry is a severe sin, just like sexual sin, and they both created havoc in my life.

Ron Mehl, a wonderful pastor now deceased, wrote a book called *The Tender Commandments*.[4] The book's back cover says, "Devoting a chapter to each commandment, Ron shows how God uses them to remove the confusion about right and wrong in today's relative culture, protect us from the consequences of our moral weakness, and guide our thinking and actions in every situation."

Were God's rules protection from the type of distress I was feeling? Were the rules I thought of as restrictive joy killers serving as protective barriers against pain?

Becket Cook gives an excellent example of this protection in a story about what his father did when his sister was a teenager.[5] She was sneaking out the window at night, so their father nailed it shut. He was trying to protect her because he loved her.

I was beginning to hear Jesus's sweet whispers and wonder if His word was accurate. I missed Jesus but was afraid life would be too hard if I left my relationship, and I'd try to follow Him and let Him down.

I couldn't imagine living without my partner. But after fighting with her a few times, I went apartment hunting. The prices were too high, however, and I didn't know if I could care for my children on one salary.

In an interview with Matt and Laurie on TBN, I heard Sheila Walsh give her testimony.[6] She described working as a national broadcaster on the 700 Club and told of her stressful childhood. Her father had committed suicide, and she felt it was her fault.

Sheila loved her work but spent hours each day with people, counseling them and always being there for them. All that stress, plus the baggage from her past, culminated in a nervous breakdown on her show.

She agreed to check herself into a psychiatric hospital to get some help. She drove herself there and came close to taking her own life on the way.

She described herself at the hospital, crouching in a corner of her room, awake the whole night. She was on suicide watch, and the staff would come and check on her frequently. She remembers a tall man standing in her doorway at 3:00 a.m. He stood there for a while, then walked over and put a little stuffed lamb in her lap. As he returned to the doorway, he said words that touched her deeply, "Your shepherd knows where you are."

Looking back, I see my Good Shepherd searching for me and gently calling my name. He is always looking for His lost sheep and wanting to bring us home.

Ezekiel 34:12–13 says it so well: *"So will I seek out My sheep and deliver them from all the places where they were scattered on a cloudy and dark day . . . and I will bring them to their own land."*

3

Coming Home

With some fear and timidity, I attended a service at a large nearby church one bright sunny Easter morning. I wasn't sure I was ready yet to return to Jesus, but I had a heart tug to be there that day. I hoped it would be a celebration like the Easters I remembered years ago.

As the worship music filled the sanctuary, I felt a happy sense of being at home. I can't remember the pastor's words, but as the service progressed, I knew I needed to give my heart to Jesus. I had left Him, and my lifestyle was wrong. I needed to return to my first love.

When we were invited to the altar to follow Jesus, I stepped out and walked tearfully down that long aisle. A man was waiting to pray with me. He listened while I asked Jesus to forgive my sins and gave Him my life. Tears streamed down my face, and a new sense of peace and joy enveloped me as His love and forgiveness washed over me.

I can't remember what I said to my partner when I got home, but I began an apartment search. I found one a few days later, gathered my children and belongings, and moved.

When I returned to Jesus and walked down that aisle, I repented and felt a new peace and joy. But as the year went on, I didn't make time to read my Bible and pray due to working, attending extra school, and raising kids. I wasn't growing in my faith, and loneliness set in. I didn't have time or take time to nourish my relationship with Jesus.

I felt cautious around Christians after leaving the gay relationship. I didn't know how to explain to anyone how I'd been living the past thirteen years. I didn't know who was safe to talk to. I even went to a women's retreat sponsored by the megachurch I was attending. The ladies must have sensed my fear because no one talked to me the whole weekend. I felt so alone.

I had heard of ex-gay groups and tried to call one but couldn't reach anyone. (There were no internet search engines in those days.) I considered going to a therapist but didn't have the money or know whom to trust to be biblical and understand my issues.

I often thought about my ex-partner and heard from friends that she also missed me. After about a year apart, I stopped by to visit her, and we fell into each other's arms. My heart was divided. Here I was, two-timing Jesus!

The year after returning to the gay relationship was terrible. We had some fun times, but our distrust and disagreements were severe. It wasn't long before I regretted my decision to move back with her, and she didn't trust me much, either. In one moment of weakness, I promised her I would never return to an evangelical church. That was a low point.

Galatians 4:9 summarizes what I had done: *"But now after you have known God, or rather are known by God, how is it that you turn again to the weak and beggarly elements, to which you desire again to be in bondage?"*

Life continued to go downhill until the day came, a year later, when I rented a U-Haul truck, packed up my kids, and moved out for good. She came home to an empty house. I wasn't in close fellowship with Jesus, but I knew I had to get out of that situation and get my life back on track. That was my turnaround day, and I never looked back. I was ready to go in a new direction.

I've learned that returning to Jesus is a "heart thing." The heart is described as the core of our being, and He changes our hearts. When I walked to that church altar a year earlier, I wanted to follow Jesus, but I didn't start to walk with Him and allow Him to change my heart.

But this time was different, and I knew I needed to follow Jesus wholeheartedly. I found a church and Portland Fellowship (an "ex-gay" ministry), where I learned to walk with Him.

Perhaps you also decided to come back to Jesus. You made that decision and enjoyed a fresh sense of joy and cleansing. It may have been a very emotional time. Or it may have been more of an intellectual decision, and you are still waiting for the feelings to catch up.

You need to know that Jesus is happy He found you and will take good care of you. I love the part in the story of the Good Shepherd when He says as He carries the little sheep home on His shoulders, *"Rejoice with me, for I have found My sheep which was lost! I say to you . . . there will be more joy in heaven over one sinner who repents than over ninety-nine just persons who need no repentance. . . . I say to you, there is joy in the presence of the angels of God over one sinner who repents"* (Luke 15:6,7,10).

Your Good Shepherd is so happy to have you home and wants you to walk closely with Him. He will heal your heart and feed you well. He will take good care of you.

Part II

Journey of Restoration

4

Healing Your Heart

The worship lifted my heart. I felt surrounded by the presence of God as we sang together at a meeting of Portland Fellowship. We were fellow travelers on the road to leaving gay relationships. Even with only twenty or thirty of us, I thought we sounded like a beautiful choir of a hundred. Tears trickled down many faces, including mine.

Our praise was deeply heartful because we had tasted the forgiveness of God. The verse about the woman who loved much and was forgiven much (Luke 7:47) came to mind. We knew we had been forgiven much.

We split into separate groups for men and women during our sharing time. There were common threads among us women as many would share how in love they had been, of relationships becoming painful, and of breakups. We were sad and confused but wanted to be right with the Lord.

We had left partners and friends (most of them left us) and sometimes jobs and possessions to follow Jesus. We were scared about the future and wondered if it would be worth all this pain.

There was a big question in my heart and others too: will we be able to stick with it? Will Jesus be enough, and will we have a happy life?

During our meetings, we studied many scriptures and learned how to apply them to our lives. It was a discipleship program composed of examining scriptures and our lives as we tried to understand what had happened to bring us to this place.

We learned that idol worship is a common trap for same-sex-attracted females, and many are prone to "love addiction." In her blog post, "The Lesbian Urge to Merge," Anne Witton describes this well:

> Lesbian relationships can be so intense and overwhelming that it's almost impossible to stop your lover from becoming God to you. This has happened to me, and it's excruciating to realize that I'd been putting someone else in God's place. It's unfair to her and ultimately unsatisfying because no other person can meet the needs in me that only God can fulfill.[1]

Idol worship can be defined as worshiping and serving *"the creature rather than the Creator"* (Romans 1:25). Ezekiel tells us what idols do to us: *"These men have set up idols in their hearts, and put before them that which causes them to stumble into iniquity . . . they are all estranged from Me by their idols"* (Ezek. 14:3,5).

The Lord also gently pointed out some other sins besides idolatry and an immoral relationship. I began to understand how much I had hurt my family, friends, and especially my children. It had taken a tremendous toll on them. This was something I learned even more about as time went on.

Looking at Roots

An important aspect we learned at Portland Fellowship is that there are often roots, stemming back to childhood, that leave us vulnerable to same-sex attraction. We had legitimate needs for love that we tried to meet illegitimately. Learning this helped us develop self-compassion and understand why these relationships can be so addicting. They came close to meeting our needs until they didn't.

Debra Fileta, a licensed counselor, wrote in her book *Reset* that looking at the roots of problems is essential. She compared it to fixing a car, that you can fix external problems, but it's important to look inside. She said, "Here's the thing about my lemon of a car ... I had to figure out what was going on underneath the surface if I wanted to turn my lemon into lemonade."[2]

Anne (Paulk) Edwards, director of Restored Hope Network, listed some possible roots for female same-sex attraction in her book *Restoring Sexual Identity*. Some of these are "childhood trauma, including incidents of sexual abuse, gender role rejection, atypical childhood play patterns, damaged mother-daughter relationships, unhealthy father-daughter relationships, and personality temperaments."[3]

Anne also mentions Dr. Elizabeth Moberly, who wrote *Homosexuality: A New Christian Ethic*. Dr. Moberly describes the need for same-sex affirmation as a "reparative drive, often an attempt to repair a missing connection with our gender."[4]

You might say many people have these kinds of issues but aren't attracted to the same sex. That is true; humans have many problems and ways to cope, which may need to be explored with a professional counselor. But the glimpses we get of deep hurts and needs in our lives provide an opportunity for prayer, forgiveness, and healing. Our women's group at Portland Fellowship provided that opportunity for me.

As we learned about these things in our group, I began to look back at my past for anything that could be thought of as roots. I didn't experience same-sex attraction during my childhood or teen years, but I did have a crush on my home economics teacher when I was about twelve or thirteen.

Then, a friendship with a Bible school student became a problem. She was thirty and I was fifteen when we began spending much time together. We often prayed and talked late into the night. She was the only one living in a Bible college dormitory next door to my home, and my parents had me live there to keep her company.

One night, I was jolted awake to realize she was lying beside me in my bed with her arm around my waist. I was afraid to move or to breathe. I knew she cared about me because she told me she could count all the most important people in her life on one hand, and I was one of them. But this and another similar episode felt romantic and created confusion that haunted me for years. That relationship seems mild compared to actual sexual abuse and terrible things that have happened to others, but it profoundly affected me.

I Need More . . .
Support to Recover

- Restored Hope Network: www.restoredhopenetwork.org
- *Restoring Sexual Identity: Hope for women who struggle with same sex attraction,* by Anne Paulk

My siblings and I were blessed to have parents who loved and cared for us, but they were students in a legalistic Bible school and had many rules: no movies, dancing, not even roller skating. My mom was especially hard on me and was often "on my case" since I was the oldest.

The saddest week of my childhood was when I was about eleven and had to give up my dog, Frisky, because she was in heat and we couldn't afford to fix her. My mom was pregnant and couldn't deal with all the dogs at the door trying to get in our house and making the snow outside yellow with their pee. I soaked my pillow every night as I cried myself to sleep. I had lost the love of my life. I tried to forgive my mom because I knew she was suffering. She was matter-of-fact about the whole thing. They were of farming stock and wanted us to be tough.

There was no hugging or coddling in our household, but I remember seeing my sister sitting on my dad's lap and wondering why he never held me. These and other clues over the years helped me understand why I might have felt a love deficit (even though I know they did love me).

Some people believe ex-gay ministries blame parents. I haven't found that to be true. Sometimes, it's simply a chemistry problem between child and parent, a mismatch between their needs and what the parent can offer.

In cases of outright sexual abuse and other traumas, it's easy to see how these needs are created. And when other problems like disrupted attachment bonds exist, the need for love can be intense.[5]

Research has also shown a high incidence of childhood sexual abuse in same-sex-attracted people. (It has been noted that treatment for issues such as this may reduce same-sex attraction as a by-product.)[6]

A continual stream of new information about same-sex attractions and possible roots exists.[7] New information over the years has provided more opportunities for healing, prayer, and forgiveness of myself and others.

Pray with and for each other

An essential part of our group prayers would be to pray with and for one another. It was freeing to bring these issues to the Lord and into the open with other sisters praying.

It's so true as it says in James 5:16 KJV, *"Confess your faults to one another, and pray for one another, that ye may be healed."* We also prayed for those who had hurt us and asked God to help us forgive them.

Prayer and sensing God's presence and the power of the Holy Spirit did much to bring joy and healing.

The Bible says God is *"near to those who have a broken heart"* (Psalm 34:18) and I did feel His closeness and forgiveness.

Jesus used the ministry of Portland Fellowship in a powerful way to begin healing my heart and provided some key insights as to roots and discipleship tools for the road ahead.

Continue in forgiveness and healing

Forgiveness and healing have continued in my life over the years as layers come off, and hurt, resentments, and various sins have been revealed. This presents fresh opportunities to ask forgiveness for myself and to pray to forgive others.

Jesus has used my church experience, the Word of God, friendships, and prayer groups to provide continued healing, which I will describe in the next chapter and throughout the book.

If you have decided to leave gay relationships and follow Jesus, I urge you to connect to a ministry in the Restored Hope Network, such as the Portland Fellowship. You might be feeling raw and unsure where to go to get the support you may need. They can also recommend counselors and other resources that can help.

Through the power of Jesus, your healing can be accomplished as described in Acts 4:10: *"Let it be known to you all, and to all the people of Israel, that by the name of Jesus Christ of Nazareth . . . this man stands before you whole."* As the Psalmist says: *"He restores my soul"* (Psalm 23:3).

Your Good Shepherd will bind up your broken heart and heal it. He will restore your soul.

5

Feeding You Well

The people in the group shared smiles and high-fives as they described their latest abortion clinic protest. I attended a Bible study with my friend, but it seemed like abortion was all they talked about. "Is this what the church should be doing?" I wondered. I felt out of place and uncomfortable. I wanted a Bible study, not politics.

Going back to church was a process. I needed spiritual food to grow, but I wasn't sure what to expect from the church and how I would be received. I felt like a weak and vulnerable lamb. I was hungry but not sure of the best place to get fed.

Feeding on the Word

Jesus tells us that He wants us to be well fed as He told His disciples three times to *"feed my lambs"* and *"feed my sheep"* (John 21:15, 17). Jesus says He feeds us by His Word: *"Man shall not live by bread alone, but by every word that proceeds from the mouth of God"* (Matt. 4:4).

I knew it was essential to find a church with sound Bible teaching where I could grow in my faith. I began attending a large church with excellent preaching and worship. Still, I left after six months because I had difficulty getting to know people. I then moved to a smaller church that was Biblically sound and stayed away from political issues.

I began to grow in the Word and felt joy as the scriptures came alive. It was a special day when I completed the new member's class and went forward to be welcomed into church membership.

During my years following Jesus since then, I have attended wonderful Bible study groups and churches under the teaching of great pastors. They have been life-giving.

My private Bible study is a vital part of my growth, and my best days are when I start with time in the Word. Words often "jump off the pages," giving me a picture of God's love, His character, and the plan of salvation. I often find words of instruction or guidance for whatever I am going through.

The past year, I started to use "The Bible Recap"[1] for my private study, a program that leads me through the Bible chronologically each year. The podcast lists the reading for each day, and then Tara-Leigh Cabell summarizes the "God shots." She also provides resources for deeper study. This program is just one of many available. I have used other Bible study programs and participated in many Bible study groups, such as Bible Study Fellowship.[2]

The internet also provides access to Bible teaching classes and other resources. In addition to Bible studies, there are great Christian apologists on YouTube—like Alisha Childers, Sean McDowell, and Dr. Michael Brown.

Learning From Others

During the early years after I came to Christ, I enjoyed reading testimonies of people who had left and avoided gay relationships to follow Christ, like Bob Davies, Andrew Comisky, Sy Rogers, and others. I loved reading their stories, and it was helpful for me to learn about their lives and how Jesus had been there for them.

I attended a national Exodus conference in those early years, and I felt encouraged by the large crowd of others who had the same struggles. I enjoyed hearing the speakers as well as meeting and hearing the stories of other attendees. I felt less alone, and it gave me hope that I could stay the course and that it would be worth it.

Growing in Worship and Prayer

Worship was and still is one of the most significant times when I've experienced the healing of the Holy Spirit. Joy and thanksgiving nourish deep parts of my heart as I soak in God's presence. (In fact, Psalm 22:3 tells us that God *"inhabits"* the praises of His people (KJV).

Prayer and prayer groups also bring a powerful sense of the presence of the Holy Spirit and growth in my faith. That includes praying alone and with others.

I have been part of a single ladies' prayer group for several years. We are from different churches, but one thing most of us have in common is that we departed from the Lord, got divorced, and later in life came back to Him. (I was the only one who had been in a gay relationship. Although they knew about it, they never asked, and I never discussed it.)

I Need More . . .

Bible Study

➢ Bible Recap Program
   thebiblerecap.com

➢ Bible Study Fellowship
   bsfinternational.org

We often pray together about our children, many of whom were not believers and we knew had been hurt by our divorces. We had all been taken in by the cultural experts who told us it was better for our children if we left an unhappy marriage. (Those experts now said they underestimated how much divorce hurts children.)[3] Praying together for our children was an opportunity to lay these burdens at His feet and accept His love and forgiveness.

The Lord tells us that as we draw near to Him, *"He will draw near to [us]"* (James 4:8). He gave us that promise, and I haven't found a better way to draw near than by prayer.

Nourishing Fellowship

When I moved and started attending a new church, a group of four of us hit it off, and we were going on a ladies' retreat where we would all be crowded together in a large house overlooking the beach. I wondered if anyone there knew about my past, and I wanted to ensure I had a private bed. I hadn't kept my past a secret but didn't talk about it openly.

One lady helped me find and set up my fold-away bed. I wondered if she and the others knew about my past. (I asked her about this recently as we are still close friends twenty-five years later and found out they did.) Looking back, I am grateful for how kind and thoughtful they were, and I believe the Lord opened their hearts toward me.

This happened with another friend I met at the same church. We often had lunch together and got to know each other well. One day, I took a blind leap and let her know about my past. She looked shocked and was quiet the rest of that day, but she burst into tears the next time I saw her and apologized for "judging" me. She said she had had a past, too, but hers involved men. Again, I felt God had provided a friend who is still a friend today.

Fellowship with friends over the years has been a vital part of my spiritual growth. An important concept in healing from same-sex attraction is that it helps to have positive affirmation from healthy same-sex relationships. The Lord has provided that over the years.

I enjoyed being a part of ministry teams traveling to other countries to do projects for many years. These projects consumed a lot of time and energy, and I had no thought of my past as the years passed; none of my friendships were problematic but were healing. I felt free and happy, growing in the Lord, and enjoying life.

How to Find a Church

The culture has dramatically changed since I came to Christ many years ago, and the gay issue now predominates. The church may seem different if you have been away from it for a while. There are a lot of confusing messages out there, and some, even evangelicals, are changing their views. Often, churches can be unsure how to act towards "ex-gay" people. You may wonder how to find a good church and if you will feel at home.

Pray and ask the Lord to help you find the right church as an essential first step. When choosing a church, it's critical to determine how they interpret the Bible. Do they use it as a literal guide, or give new meanings to words such as "inspired" and "salvation"?

Progressive churches often have a political agenda and are not focused on sharing the gospel and training believers. They will not provide you with spiritual food or *"correctly explain the Word of truth"* (2 Tim. 2:15 NLT).

One way to vet a church is to talk to someone in their leadership and read their website to determine their stance on the gay issue. If you see a gay flag hanging on their door, walk right by. That is usually a good clue about their stance on Biblical integrity. Many who call themselves "welcoming" and "affirming" no longer hold a traditional view of Biblical morality.

You can always ask for recommendations if you have friends who are solid believers. You can also check with the Restored Hope Network to see if they know of good churches in your area.

You might be nervous to get to know Christians personally and feel like keeping them at arm's length for a while. I understand, but I encourage you to take the plunge and join your new church's social activities. Your church and other gatherings of believers will provide a great source of fellowship that will nourish you.

It's wise to share your story with your pastor and a few trusted others until you get to know people and their feelings about this issue. There is such a wide range of reactions that it's wise to take your time.

The Holy Spirit has been described as a comforter and teacher; I have found that to be true. The love of Jesus is communicated so powerfully by the Holy Spirit through the Word, worship, and fellowship with others. Jesus has provided these ways to feed you, and I encourage you to use them. Keep your eyes and ears open to where He will lead you to be fed, to the people He will send your way, and remember to do your part in faithfully reading His word.

Ezekiel 34:15 says, *"'I will feed My flock, and I will make them lie down,' says the Lord GOD."* These scriptures show God's heart for us, and I encourage you to let your shepherd feed and nourish you back to health.

Your Good Shepherd will feed you well!

6

Support If You Fall

Close calls are virtually all alike. They begin with an attraction to somebody other than your spouse that causes you to think about your time with this individual simply for the pleasure that it provides you. Maybe you have regular meetings with someone of the opposite sex for business, shared interests, or volunteer opportunities.

In other words, you start to daydream about this person. It is not just the thought "Boy, is he good looking," or "Wow, she's gorgeous," but rather it is the reflection on the individual that results from the initial contact.

Somewhere in this phase, a mere friendship ceases and a close call starts. Now you're saving topics of conversation for this person. Your conversation ranges from topics related to your mutual interest to far-ranging ones—and soon into personal issues. This reflection on personal life will cultivate the relationship. You scheme and plan on how to be together more often, for more time, without raising anyone's suspicion."

~ Dave Carder, *Anatomy of an Affair*

***D**ave Carder is a pastor* with forty years of experience listening to stories of marital unfaithfulness, many among believers, including church leaders and pastors.

Dave explains that "stuff you brought with you" can be part of the vulnerabilities that make one susceptible.[1] These include issues like sexual molestation and other areas of family dysfunction, which are many of the same problems that affect same-sex-attracted people.

I had a close call in the first year or two after returning to Christ. A woman in my church was going through a divorce and we began to spend much time together. Her face lit up whenever she saw me, and she sought my advice. She seemed to need and want my support in dealing with her divorce issues. She had no experience in the working world and worried about providing for herself and her children.

After a few months, I began thinking about her often and looking forward to time with her. It wasn't a romantic attraction at first but a matter of enjoying her affirmation and wanting to spend more and more time with her.

One night, I was at her house, and she started crying over her divorce. She was sitting on a chair, her body shaking, and her face was in her hands. I just wanted to wrap my arms around her. But something stopped me. Hugs are usually no problem for me, except for a couple of times, and I knew this was one. A warning signal in my head told me that an attraction was starting to build.

This caused me to have a conversation with my pastor. He told me to stay away from her, but unfortunately, I didn't listen. She needed a friend, and I was afraid to leave her. It felt good to help her, and I thought I could handle it.

We talked on the phone almost every day, and thinking about her began to take up much space in my head. I would rehash our conversations in my mind and wonder how she was doing all through the day.

Another night, I was at her house, and heavy snow fell. She invited me to stay over because she worried about me driving home. As she tucked me into bed in her guest room, I reached out my arms to her. She pulled away, saying she wanted to be close but was afraid. I also wanted to be close. It was a close call.

I cried the next day when I returned home and looked at the beautiful sky over the barn and trees in my backyard. "Lord, how could I let you down," I thought. "Please forgive me." But I didn't feel forgiven.

I was reading my Bible a day or two later when I just "happened" to read a passage that jumped off the pages:

> *Now Joshua was clothed with filthy garments and was standing before the Angel. Then He answered and spoke to those who were standing before Him saying, "Take away the filthy garments from him." And to him He said, "See, I have removed your iniquity from you, and I will clothe you with rich robes." And I said, "Let them put a clean turban on his head." So they put a clean turban on his head, and they put the clothes on him. And the angel of the Lord stood by.*
>
> Zechariah 3:3–5

The tears flowed as I read that. I felt a sense of release and forgiveness. That scripture reassured me that Jesus had seen it and had forgiven me. That was the closest I came to falling, but there was another time years later when hugs gave me trouble.

Be aware of warning signs

God has provided many friendships that have brought joy and healing into my life. But I have had to deal with some warning signs in two or three friendships over my thirty-plus years of following Jesus.

In those two or three friendships, after many years, it seemed like a switch flipped out of the blue, and I suddenly found myself thinking about them all the time and wanting to get together. There was never physical involvement or a desire for any, but if I was honest, I had to admit something was wrong.

Christopher Yuan describes in his book *Holy Sexuality* that a relationship is off-kilter when "throughout the day you ponder, *Does she miss me right now?* Your thoughts are fixated on planning out details of what you'll next do with him.... You cry for days if the relationship changes or ends."[2]

Looking back, I can see my feelings were triggered by the friendship changing due to geographical moves or my choices to spend more time with others. But I found myself in great grief and even drove past someone's house twice or thrice to see if her car was there. That's how bad it got.

I eventually understood that these relationships had become codependent even though each was different. Lori Rentzel Thorkelson, in *Emotional Dependency and How to Keep Your Friendships Healthy*, states that emotional dependency is when "the ongoing presence and nurturing of another is believed to be necessary for personal security."[3]

When these situations arose, I knew I needed to admit that these relationships had drifted into dangerous territory. Rosaria Butterfield, in describing the danger of sin, says it's like bringing a baby tiger into your home and putting a collar and a leash on her "and naming her 'Fluffy'." Rosaria says: "Don't be surprised you wake up one day and Fluffy is eating you alive."[4] Her message is a good one: It's dangerous, don't even bring it into the house!

It was time for an action plan!

Put your action plan in place

Lori Thorkelson Rentzel's booklet has been my go-to resource when these situations arise. I probably read it forty times or more during those difficult times of breaking free. I love that her booklet is based on Biblical principles, realistic descriptions of the situations, and action steps to take. Here is a summary of some of her points, which I have adapted.

1. Acknowledge it as sin

Lori says it's often hard to see these things as sin, and it's easy to deceive oneself when you have a Christian friend, and there has been no physical involvement or even a desire for one.

Lori states that we all have a deep need, placed in us by God, for intimate fellowship[5] and then lists some of the signs that a healthy friendship has crossed the line into emotional dependency[6] and some issues that make us vulnerable.[7]

2. Deal with the relationship

Lori states that it is vital to distance oneself from a friendship once it becomes codependent.[8] This may mean not having contact or being together only in group settings for a long time; months, or maybe years. This part is so hard. But I've learned that though challenging, it is worth it.

The wise counsel from Lori and others is never to let the person know you are overly attached and why you are distancing yourself.[9] That's one of the most challenging parts because I never want to hurt a friend.

A friend told me a story that helped those times. She has a daughter who was into drugs, and she worried about her constantly. One day, she was at her desk and heard the Lord say, "I love Janet more than you do." Remembering that helps the process of letting go. When I start to worry about my friend obsessively, I turn those thoughts into prayers that God will bless her, and it helps to know He loves her more than I do.

3. Expect a time of grieving

The grieving time can be excruciating. During periods of letting go, I've found it helps to spend extra time in the Word, in worship, and with other Christian friends. I have found that this is a great time to reach out and make new friends or to spend more time with those I have. It can also be an excellent time to sign up for a new class or do something fun I've been putting off. It's hard to let go at first, but it gets easier over time.

4. Ask for help

I have found that when I cry out to Jesus, He comes to the rescue. I may not feel His presence immediately, but as I keep crying out, He will send things like a comforting song, a scriptural promise, or an encouraging word from a friend to let me know He is near.

Of course, it's always good to share and have prayer with a pastor or prayer partner when possible.

I have found it challenging to share with others during these times due to privacy issues. Christian prayer hotlines like June Hunt's "Hope for the Heart"[10] and "Focus on the Family"[11] are places to pray confidentially with someone about these situations. Focus on the Family also provides one free counseling session and has a list of Christian counselors. Another source of help is local ministries through the Restored Hope Network,[12] and some churches have counselors or referral networks.

Two times during these struggles, I scheduled appointments with a good Christian counselor who believes in traditional Biblical morality. It just took a few visits, but it helped a lot.

5. Gain understanding

I often wonder when caught up in one of these dependencies why they have so much power over me. It's good to reflect on possible roots—often I rediscover the information that helps. I recently learned that women have hormones that can make love addicting. This kind of knowledge lends objectivity to the situation.

Remember, often these dependencies are based upon a legitimate unmet need for love, which reminds us to look to God to meet those needs in His way.

6. Do the opposite thing

Ephesians 4:28 tells the thief to no longer steal but to do the opposite thing and earn money so *"that he may have something to give him who has need."* That reminds me that instead of worshiping a person, I can do the opposite thing and pour all that love to the Lord. As I express my love to Him in praise and worship, His love feels more tangible.

7. *Walk closely with the Lord*

This book will provide you with some specifics on how to do that. I've found that the best solution to these problems is to walk closely in step with Him. Then, my heart is sensitive to those little nudges from the Holy Spirit, and He gives me the strength to make the right choices.

8. *Get help with deeper healing*

In those early years of my walk with Christ, I discovered the booklet *Freedom in Christ* by Neil Anderson, which—along with its accompanying workbook—provides a pattern for deliverance from strongholds.[13]

It has checklists with a wide range of questions such as: Have I been exposed to Ouija boards? Is there anyone I need to forgive? Neil provides specific prayers for deliverance from unforgiveness and other issues that cause problems in one's life. I found this a beneficial exercise to pray through and break any connections or soul ties in my heart that hold me back from freedom.

9. *Keep things in perspective*

It's easier to walk through these things knowing you have been through them before, and He has brought you through. It helps to keep me on track when I look back and realize what a disaster it would have been to slip into codependency.

While helping at a community garden the other day, the leader had me plant some small delicate kale starts. Often two little plants (about an inch tall each) were intertwined. She quietly said they would do better if separated. It was no easy task, as they were so tiny and entangled, but I did what she asked, knowing each would be healthier. As I worked with those tiny vines, I thought, "What a vivid illustration of codependency!"

Be prepared for joy

My transparency may make you think I have suffered greatly in these last thirty-five years of following Jesus. Looking back, there was some suffering in those codependencies, but they have only taken up about three or four of those years of my life.

Although there was a little cloud over those years, they were still marked by much joy and beautiful times of walking with the Lord.

There is extra joy after getting through a time of testing. Whenever one of these problems came up, I knew He had brought me through it before and would do so again. I knew that He kept me *"from stumbling"* (Jude 1:24) and I would find joy on the other side.

I Need More . . .

Who Am I?

- Holy Sexuality <u>holysexuality.com</u>
- *Restoring Sexual Identity: Hope for women who struggle with same sex attraction,* by Anne Paulk
- *Emotional Dependency and How to Keep Your Friendships Healthy,* by Lori Thorkelson Rentzel.

The wonderful thing is that these friendships no longer have an unhealthy hold on my heart and have been restored over time. The Lord does make all things new.

He will do the same for you, and it's worth going through these steps. You won't regret it. I want you to know that Jesus will bring you out and will give you the power to say no. Ezekiel describes it beautifully: *"They shall be safe in their land; and they shall know that I am the LORD, when I have broken the bands of their yoke and delivered them from the hands of those who enslaved them"* (Ezek. 34:27).

Your Good Shepherd will set you free and put a "new song" in your mouth (Psalm 40:3).

7

Dealing with Opposition

We were huddled together inside the church. The people outside were screaming as they banged on the windows, and it was hard to hear our speakers sharing about the healing Jesus was doing in their lives. I was at a Portland Fellowship conference where we listened to testimonies from people who had found Jesus and left same-sex relationships.

The screaming people were gay activists who weren't happy about the conference. My stomach felt tight as I listened. Why were they so angry at us? We were working on our own lives and weren't hurting anyone. Then I remembered my anger when I screamed at those picketing Christians a few years earlier. It still felt terrible and was a taste of worse things to come.

I thought of my friends who had left me since I decided to follow Jesus. All of them had ended our friendship, some more kindly than others. Most of them I had known for at least ten years and had been there for them in their good times and bad. I told them about my new relationship with Jesus and the changes in my life. I wasn't asking them to change, but they were still upset. As one of them told me, "I don't even want to know anyone who thinks like you do."

Expect Opposition

This past year, I was studying the books of Ezra and Nehemiah and learning about their projects of rebuilding Jerusalem and its walls. It was interesting to see how the enemy attacked and how they resisted. I could see how the enemy's tactics paralleled what the enemy tries to do to us when God is rebuilding our lives.

Be aware of enemy tactics

Enemies started attacking Nehemiah and the people when they first began rebuilding the walls of Jerusalem, and some of their tactics included:

- **Angry Outbursts** *"When Sanballat heard that we were rebuilding the wall, that he was furious and very indignant . . . And he spoke before his brethren . . . and said, 'What are these feeble Jews doing?'"* (Neh. 4:1–2).

- **Mocking** *"Whatever they build, if even a fox goes up on it, he will break down their stone wall"* (Neh. 4:3).

- **Making Afraid** *"For they all were trying to make us afraid, saying, 'Their hands will be weakened in the work, and it will not be done'"* (Neh. 6:9).

- **Creating Confusion** *"When Sanballat . . . heard that the walls of Jerusalem were being restored and the gaps were beginning to be closed, . . . they became very angry, and all of them conspired together to come attack Jerusalem and create confusion"* (Neh. 4:7–8).

Maybe that's what the people beating on our church windows were trying to do—discourage us and make us afraid. We all had fears we couldn't do it, fears it wouldn't be worth it, and fears we would let Jesus down, and that wall banging didn't help. Then we heard confusing voices saying it's okay to live in gay relationships and that we are not being true to ourselves.

Guard against personal attacks

Nehemiah tells us that Sanballat became more aggressive as more progress was made. When the other tactics failed, he gathered his forces to surround and physically attack the builders. He said they would *"come into their midst and kill them and cause the work to cease"* (Neh. 4:11).

This didn't succeed either, so Sanballat directed his attacks against Nehemiah's person. He tried to kill him when the walls were complete and all that needed to be done was hanging the windows. Nehemiah related that when Sanballat and his minions *"heard that I had rebuilt the wall, and that there were no breaks left in it ... [they] sent to me, saying, 'Come, let us meet together' ... But they thought to do me harm"* (Neh. 6:1-2). Then Nehemiah was warned *"for they are coming to kill you"* (Neh. 6:10).

It interested me that the attacks were directed at Nehemiah personally when the project was almost complete. I've also noticed some personal attacks since sharing my testimony more openly in the past two years.

Even though I haven't been physically attacked, I spent some sleepless nights about a year ago.

It all started when I learned the elementary school near me was having a "kid pride" parade featuring some drag queens, and a few of us had a prayer walk around the school a few days before the event. Two ladies had signs with "Jesus is the Way, the Truth, and the Life" written on them.

We met on a corner near the school after the walk to pray again, and that's when people started screaming at us and taking pictures. Some shouted from cars, some came out of their houses, and others were on the sidewalk.

A few days later, I got a call from the police, which started my sleepless nights. When I got the call, I was riding in a car and couldn't hear well, but the person said they were "Officer ..." I hung up on them. I thought maybe it was a scam.

My mind began racing. I figured it had to be because of our prayer walk and protests at the school. After that first call, I got several "restricted" calls in the next few days, and I became increasingly afraid that the police were calling me to interview me thinking I was a "domestic terrorist."

I didn't sleep better until I called the police department to ask if they would ever call without leaving a message, and they said no, they wouldn't. Praying with others also calmed my spirit.

Some of my family members are very liberal and disagree with me on this and other issues, such as the gay issue. Some college-age ones will barely speak to me.

During this time, an older family member, who often says negative things to me, said, "You think you are superior, don't you?" Wow, that felt up close and personal, and it made me realize some pride had crept in to damage my witness.

These reactions felt like a slap in the face. Honestly, a lot of anger and unforgiveness crept into my heart. These feelings were so intense I felt like a bad Christian. I felt far away from God and wondered if He had done any work in my life. I felt like a failure.

Yes, I was partly to blame, but after I read about Nehemiah's story, I realized that part of it was the enemy's attack. He was mad because God had been working in my life, not because He hadn't been.

Prepare for Battle

It encouraged me to see how Ezra and Nehemiah responded to these attacks and what the outcome was. It gives a good template for preparing for the battles we will face as we follow Jesus.

- Confess all sin. Nehemiah started confessing his people's sins when he first heard about the walls being broken down. *"I pray before You now, day and night, . . . and confess the sins of the children of Israel which we have sinned against You. . . . We have acted very corruptly against You, and have not kept the commandments"* (Neh. 1:6–7).

    Ezra also approached God with a confession of sin: *"Now while Ezra was praying, and while he was confessing, weeping, and bowing down before the house of God"* (Ezra 10:1).

- **Pray and fast.** Ezra 9 and Nehemiah 9 record extensive prayer with fasting by both men. My study Bible states, "Prayer and fasting are mentioned multiple times as they set out on tasks, and the whole rebuilding of the wall was bathed in prayer. Prayer is combined with action through Nehemiah, and both books underscore the need to approach God constantly in prayer."[1]

- **Worship.** Worship was part of the rebuilding process from the very beginning. Ezra lists singers as among the returning exiles. The people had a worship service as they cleared the land and began to lay the foundations. *"The priests stood in their apparel with trumpets, and the Levites . . . with cymbals, to praise the Lord . . . they sang responsively, praising and giving thanks to the* LORD. *'For He is good. For His mercy endures forever toward Israel.' Then all the people shouted with a loud shout . . . because the foundation of the house of the Lord was laid"* (Ezra 3:10–11).

- **Be Watchful.** Nehemiah was proactive in setting up a watch day and night when Sanballat surrounded them with armies, *"We made a prayer to our God, and because of them set a watch against them day and night"* (Neh. 4:9).

    This theme is repeated In the New Testament when Peter reminds us to be watchful. *"Be sober, be vigilant; because your adversary the devil walks about like a roaring lion, seeking whom he may devour"* (1 Pet. 5:8).

- **Have your weapons ready.** Nehemiah made sure the builders and the people had their weapons in place. *"Every one of the builders had his sword girded at his side as he built"* (Neh. 4:18).

Paul tells us in Ephesians 6:11–17 to wear our spiritual armor and to *"take . . . the sword of the Spirit, which is the word of God."* A sword is a powerful offensive weapon, and we are told *"the weapons of our warfare . . . are mighty in God for pulling down strongholds"* (2 Cor. 10:4). The word of God is your sword, your powerful spiritual weapon.

When in the Battle

These books give us good examples of how to respond effectively in battle, to warfare we don't expect or ask for. Here is a summary of what they did and what we can do.

- Ask God for help. From the beginning and throughout their projects, Ezra and Nehemiah asked God for help. Nehemiah specifically asks God to *"strengthen my hands"* (Nehemiah 6:9, 8:20).

- Don't be afraid. Nehemiah reminded them of God's power when the enemy's opposition was great. *"Do not be afraid of them. Remember the Lord great and awesome, and fight"* (Neh. 4:14).

- Work together. Nehemiah gave the people different tasks so they could help each other. He split them with one half guarding the weapons and one half working. *"From that time on, that half of my servants worked at construction, while the other half held the spears, the shields, the bows, and wore armor"* (Neh. 4:16).

  Nehemiah placed the family groups along the wall and gave each family a little trumpet they could blow when they got overwhelmed so other people would know to come and help them (Neh. 4:19–20).

- Let Him fight for you. The trumpets let them know their friends were in trouble, but Nehemiah also told them the trumpets would remind them that *"our God will fight for us"* (Neh. 4:20). He wanted to make sure they recognized that the battle belonged to the Lord. (David also recognized this before he fought Goliath as recorded in 1 Sam. 17:37.)

  Sanballat and his minions even recognized that it was the God of the Israelites Who defeated them. *"And it happened, when our enemies heard that it was known to us, and that God had brought their plot to nothing, that all of us returned to the wall, everyone to his work"* (Neh. 4:15).

Celebrate the Victory

The people of Israel *"celebrated . . . with joy"* when Ezra completed the temple (Ezra 6:16). Then, when Nehemiah completed the wall, they brought out the Levites *"to celebrate the dedication with gladness, both with thanksgivings and singing, with cymbals and stringed instruments and harps"* (Neh. 12:27).

Nehemiah even had two choirs giving thanks (Neh. 12:40), and the celebration was so grand that *"the joy of Jerusalem was heard afar off"* (Neh. 12:43).

Nehemiah was able to get the wall built in fifty-two days! That was record time, and it says even their enemies gave credit to God. *"When all our enemies heard of it, and all the nations around us saw these things, . . . they were very disheartened in their own eyes; for they perceived that this work was done by our God"* (Neh. 6:16).

Over and over through the building process, Nehemiah reached out to God for help and gave Him the credit. God was the one who won the battle! And as Nehemiah says, *"Our God will fight for us"* (Neh. 4:20).

One day, when I felt attacked, I did what we were told not to do—open the Bible and see what verse struck our eye. But I felt desperate, so I did it. I opened my Bible to Psalm 59:9. *"I will wait for You, O You his Strength, for God is my defense."*

That verse comforted me and renewed my faith. It helped me realize that even though I couldn't see Him, God was in the background taking care of things. I felt a new sense of joy as well. As it says in Nehemiah 8:10b, *"For the joy of the LORD is your strength."*

You may go through opposition, and it may increase the more you follow Christ, but He has given you tools and the knowledge that He will fight for you. I trust that you can refer to these stories of Ezra and Nehemiah to encourage you and help you know how to respond.

David tells us in Psalm 23:4 that he fears no evil because his Good Shepherd is with him. He also states in Psalm 23:5 that his Good Shepherd will anoint his head with oil and prepare for him a table in the presence of his enemies. Your Good Shepherd will do that for you too and you can relax, knowing that He's got this!

Your Good Shepherd loves you, and He will protect you.

8

Evading Deception, Traps, and Detours

*C*hristopher Yuan accepted Christ while in prison for drug use. He had lived as a gay man for many years; he wanted to follow Christ and keep living as he had been. He was elated when the chaplain gave him a book that affirmed gay relationships for Christians, thinking he would love nothing more, but after reading only half the book he returned it to the chaplain. Although a new believer, his own Bible study proved that the book falsely interpreted the Bible.[1] Christopher loved reading the Bible and went on to earn his Doctorate in Biblical Studies at Moody Bible Institute, where he taught for many years.

> ### *I Need More . . .*
> **by Christopher Yuan**
>
> ➤ *Holy Sexuality and the Gospel: Sex, Desire, and Relationships Shaped by God's Grand Story*
>
> ➤ The Holy Sexuality Project, holysexuality.com. His recently completed video series for youth

You may face all kinds of deceptive voices, traps, and detours as you follow Jesus. I want to share some of them with you and how you can trust Jesus to keep you from them.

You might hear deceptive voices

"Revoice" is a group that provides networking for people with Christian beliefs and same-sex attractions. There are two groups of people in today's world that call themselves "Side A," with members who believe it's okay for Christians to live in monogamous gay relationships, and "Side B," with members who stick to the biblical view that sexual activity is only appropriate in a male/female traditional marriage. Revoice agrees with "Side B" and they have conferences, podcasts, and other events and refer to themselves as "gay Christians."

The sad thing about groups like Revoice is that they use confusing labels and offer little hope for change. Beckett Cook has produced a YouTube video titled, "There is no such thing as a Gay Christian." Rosaria Butterfield and Christopher Yuan are his guests, and they explain that this terminology is unbiblical, that Side A is incompatible with the Christian faith, and that Side B uses non-Biblical labels.[2]

Many Christian young people are beginning to believe it's okay to be gay because of groups like this and progressive leaders and teachers. They want to be loving and affirming but are drifting away from Biblical truth.

Some people grew up as Christians but went into gay relationships and began to loudly proclaim that it's okay to be gay and Christian. Executive Director Jason Thompson of Portland Fellowship told me men have admitted to him that even though they lived as openly gay for many years and adamantly said it was okay to be gay during that time, they knew in their hearts it wasn't true.

Progressive leaders and teachers produce results like the false shepherds described by Ezekiel who did not feed the flock: *"The weak you have not strengthened, nor have you healed those who were sick, nor bound up the broken, nor brought back what was driven away, nor sought what was lost"* (Ezek. 34:4).

Jesus described false shepherds as *"thieves and robbers"* (John 10:8). He also called them wolves in sheep's clothing (Matt.

7:15). In *The Bait of Satan*, John Bevere wrote, "Wolves always go after the wounded young sheep, not the healthy strong ones. These wolves will tell people what they want to hear, not what they need to hear."[3]

He will lead you to the truth

In contrast, Jesus said: *"You shall know the truth, and the truth shall make you free"* (John 8:32). We receive the Holy Spirit when we decide to follow Jesus, and the Holy Spirit will *"guide you into all truth"* (John 16:13).

Jesus warned about deception four times in Matthew 24, and He describes what to expect before He returns at the end of the age. Jesus said those who are His sheep *"will by no means follow a stranger, but will flee from him, for they do not know the voice of strangers"* (John 10:5).

Discernment is another name for recognizing the truth. Charles Spurgeon says that discernment is not knowing the difference between right and wrong but knowing the difference between "right and almost right."[4]

Christopher Yuan could recognize what was "almost right" even as a new believer because he read his Bible a lot. The Bible tells us that regular time in the Word ("solid food") will increase our discernment. *"Solid food belongs to those who . . . by reason of use have their senses exercised to discern both good and evil"* (Heb. 5:14).

Watch their lives

When Jesus warned against false prophets and wolves masquerading in sheep's clothing, He added: *"You will know them by their fruits"* (Matt. 7:16).

When I wandered morally, I began to question and reinterpret the Bible. This is often the case with many theologians deconstructing or making public pronouncements of their changing views. They are usually going through a divorce or other significant changes in their lives at the same time.

Alisa Childers says many of these false teachers spread ideas that haven't stood the test of time to see how they affect people's lives. They do not know how these ideas will work out in the long run, yet they tell others to follow their example. She says their advice is "frequently based upon recent life-altering decisions that seem to make them happy in the moment but haven't stood the test of time."[5]

Alisa mentions Glennan Doyle, a woman once a famous Christian blogger, who tells the story of leaving her husband for another woman in her book *Unchained*. Glennan compared herself to a caged cheetah at a zoo and decided to break out of her domesticated prison. She believes it makes her a good role model for her children to put her own needs first.[6] I would be interested to hear from Glennan several years after she has had the opportunity to look at the long-term impact of that choice for herself and her children.

> ### *I Need More . . .*
> **About Traps and Deception**
>
> ➤ *Five Lies of Our Antichristian Age,* by Rosaria Butterfield.
>
> *Live Your Truth and Other Lies: Exposing Popular Deceptions that Make Us Anxious, Exhausted, and Self-Obsessed,* by Alisha Childers.

You might feel like complaining

It is easy to fall into a complaining trap when we forget all that God has done. I often need to think about the big picture when something goes wrong.

I have learned a lot from the example of the children of Israel complaining against Moses in the wilderness. *"Why is it you have brought us up out of Egypt, to kill us and our children and our livestock with thirst?"* (Exod. 17:3).

The people not only complained but *"they soon forgot His works; They did not wait for His counsel"* (Ps. 106:13). And so, God sent *"leanness to their soul"* (Ps. 106:15). They lost their joy by complaining and not waiting for His advice.

It's been easy for me to start complaining to myself when I know I must give up a friendship. As mentioned, sometimes it seems unfair, especially when the relationship has been aboveboard. I have learned to stop, ask for His advice, and not resist what He tells me to do.

It makes it so much easier to do this when I remember how He has helped me in previous times and how grateful I've been. It's a blessing to see these friendships eventually restored to a healthy place, even though, in some cases, years later.

You might be tempted by the trap of offense or detour of hard things

When you decide to follow Christ, you might feel that God promises everything to be rosy and easy, which can be confusing when hard things come up. You probably have experienced much joy in following Christ, but sometimes things might seem hard. You might feel you have given up much to follow Christ and don't know what to think.

The Trap of Offense

Offense is one of the most challenging things to deal with, especially from other believers.

People with a church background may remember good experiences but also carry some baggage. As someone who grew up in church, I have happy memories and had a good experience returning to church, even though I feared how I would be accepted.

The culture has dramatically changed since I came to Christ many years ago, and the gay issue now predominates. There are a lot of confusing messages out there, and some—even evangelicals—are changing their views. Many people are uncomfortable with the issue.

Recently, as I've been more public with my story, I've had negative reactions from a few Christians I had just met who didn't know me. They wouldn't make eye contact and walked away to avoid a conversation. That hurt a lot, but it helped me cope to remember all the years of believers reacting in kind and loving ways.

It also helped me to think of those whose harsh reactions softened over time. Recently when I felt rejected, others came alongside and were kind and helpful. In one case, someone invited me to her home to join her family for dinner. It felt as if the Lord sent some angels my way.

John Bevere also discusses this in his book. The premise is that the evil one is using personal offenses to divide and trap believers.[7] The Lord has promised us that His heart is to care for us. Sometimes, I may feel rejected or offended, but I try to keep my eyes on Him and pay attention to the angels He sends.

Detour of Hard Things

It may be difficult to tell if the hard things we go through are from Satan or a time of testing that the Lord may allow. I discussed various tactics of Satan in Chapter 7, but we know from the scriptures that the Lord may also allow testing times.

I recently listened to a podcast by Andrew Brunson, a missionary who was held in a Turkish prison for two years. He said he didn't feel God's presence during that time and was almost broken several times. He tried to worship, pray, and study his Bible each day, and he even tried to dance before the Lord, but he never felt God's presence. He said he was carried through by previous years of good experiences with God. God had prepared his heart for the hard times.[8]

It has helped me to learn from scripture that sometimes God tests us to see "what is in our heart." Examples such as the Book of Job describe this at length. Deuteronomy 8:2 tells us explicitly that the children of Israel were being tested in the wilderness. *"And you shall remember that the Lord your God led you all the way these forty years in the wilderness, to humble you and test you, to know what was in your heart."*

Deuteronomy 8:3 says He wanted them to know *"that man shall not live by bread alone, but . . . by every word that proceeds from the mouth of the LORD."*

We are instructed to rejoice in these times of testing.

> *In this you greatly rejoice, though now for a little while, if need be, you have been grieved by various trials, that the genuineness of your faith, being much more precious than gold that perishes, though it is tested by fire, may be found to praise, honor, and glory at the revelation of Jesus Christ, whom having not seen you love.*
>
> 1 Peter 1:6–8

Wow, that's a lot—to go through hard times and rejoice in them. But it helps to know it will honor the Lord.

You need to prepare your heart

Andrew Brunson feels God may have been testing his endurance in prison so he could share with others to prepare their hearts. He believes Americans could be entering a time of persecution and increasing difficulty and recommends we prepare our hearts while we have the opportunity.[9]

Andrew says we should spend as much time in the Word as possible as well as experience the joy of the Lord in worship and fellowship with other believers. These things can build up reserves to draw from during dry and difficult times. In 2 Chronicles 19:3 King Jehoshaphat was told: *"Nevertheless good things are found in you, in that you have removed the wooden images from the land, and have prepared your heart to seek God."*

Have you run into some bumps along the way? Have there been times when the Lord seems distant, and hard and difficult things are happening to you? It will help you to read the stories and promises in scripture and to learn about the experiences of others in our time to encourage you and help you endure.

I Need More . . .

To Prepare My Heart

➢ "Prepare to Stand" by Andrew Brunson. Session 1 "Recognize the Danger" Session 3 "Guarding against the Offended Heart" www.epc.org/preparetostand

It will be good to prepare your heart. Remember, Jesus will help you through it. He is there with you and will make a way as you lean upon His Word, the promises He has given, and what He has shown you through the lives of others in Scripture.

Ezekiel 34:25-26 describes David being set up as a shepherd over the people (Bible scholars say this is a type of Christ), doing beautiful things for his people. *"I will make a covenant of peace with them, and cause wild beasts to cease from the land, and they will dwell safely in the wilderness and sleep in the woods. I will make them and the places round about My hill a blessing; and I will cause showers to come down in their season; there shall be showers of blessing."*

Jesus makes this very personal in John 10:27-28: *"My sheep hear My voice and I know them, and they follow Me. And I give them eternal life, and they shall never perish; neither shall anyone snatch them out of My hand."*

Your Good Shepherd will bring you out of trouble and take good care of you.

Part III

Doing Your Part

9

Walk Closely with Jesus

Our van stopped suddenly, and we piled out. The bridge ahead had collapsed, and a railroad trestle was the only way across the river that was two or three hundred feet below.

Our ministry group in Cambodia was on our way back to base camp after a day helping locals build a church in their village when we encountered a surging mass of people near the trestle. It felt like we were on a movie set. Many of them were dressed in ethnic clothing; others looked like farmers wearing worn, ill-fitting, and soiled clothes. We made our way down a steep dirt slope to join them.

"How can we make it over that bridge?" I wondered. The trestle had very little room on each side of the railroad tracks, and two groups of people walked over the tracks, one in each direction. Most people carried bundles of clothing, food, or cooking pots on their backs, arms, or heads. Others were holding tires, car parts, or other large mechanical objects. It looked iffy, at best, that we could make it over.

Our team leader lined us up for the crossing with one person in front and one behind each of us. The one in front of me was young and strong, the one behind me a more petite teenager. As we walked across the bridge, we put our hand on the shoulder of the person in front of us. It was comforting to have that human touch, but I knew we would all go down if one fell. I couldn't look at the river below. "Please, Lord, help us do this," I thought.

I prayed with each step across that bridge, focusing all my attention on my feet, relying on the person in front of me and behind me to keep steady. It seemed as if it took forever, but we made it over. Everyone smiled and laughed as we reached solid ground and returned to our base.

I had dinner with some good friends and prayer partners when I got home from the trip. I told them about crossing the bridge. One friend's eyes got large and shiny as I shared the story. Then she told us she had prayed for me while I was on the trip. She said she got a visual image of my feet and prayed, "Lord, guide Leslie step by step by step." We all looked at each other with surprise and joy at how specifically God had guided her prayer.

This is a friend that often gets a "word" from God. She got the word "pandemic" a few months before the COVID virus hit. She wasn't even sure what it meant. Another word was "eschatological," which she had to look up. (A few days later her pastor started a study of Revelation and she learned it meant "concerning future events.")

I know that this friend spends much time in Bible study and prayer, and her heart is sensitive to hearing words from God. She listens for His voice.

Why is it important to hear God's voice?

Learning to hear God's voice has been essential in my walk with Jesus. Despite stops and starts along the way, it has made all the difference when I take the time to hear from Him. He gently tells me what to do and, most importantly, what I shouldn't do.

In his book *Whisper: How to Hear the Voice of God*, Mark Batterson says,

> Nothing has the potential to change your life like the whisper of God. Nothing will determine your destiny more than your ability to hear His still small voice. That's how you discern the good, pleasing, and perfect will of God.[1]

He wants to be close to you

It may seem surprising, but the scriptures tell us that God wants to be close to us. Enoch is a Biblical character who pleased God so much that he "*did not see death, 'and was not found because God had taken him'*" (Heb. 11:5). Enoch is described as walking "*in habitual fellowship with God*" (Gen. 5:22 AMP).

Mark Batterson also says:

> When someone speaks in a whisper you have to get very close to hear. We lean toward a whisper and that's what God wants. The goal of hearing the heavenly Father's voice isn't just hearing His voice, it's intimacy with Him. That's why He speaks in a whisper. He wants to be as close to us as divinely possible! He loves us, likes us, that much.[2]

He wants to give you instructions

Moses and King David are two other examples of men who walked closely with God and followed His instructions. God describes Moses as "*faithful in all my house. I speak with him face to face*" (Num. 12:7–8). King David was also devoted to God to do His will, and God described him this way: "*My servant David, who kept My commandments and who followed Me with all his heart, to do only what was right in My eyes*" (1 Ki. 14:8b).

Isaiah tells us about how specific directions from God can be. "*Your ears shall hear a word behind you, saying, 'This is the way, walk in it,' Whenever you turn to the right hand Or whenever you turn to the left*" (Is. 30:21).

He wants to give you warnings

Since leaving the gay relationship, I have become increasingly aware of God's voice, and I take more time to listen for it. It has been that still, quiet voice that has kept me out of trouble a few times. I've been vulnerable to getting off track when I've allowed His voice to grow dim.

Oswald Chambers describes it well in *My Utmost for His Highest*:

> The voice of the Spirit of God is as gentle as a summer breeze—so gentle that unless you are living in complete fellowship and oneness with God you will never hear it. The sense of warning and restraint that the Spirit gives comes to us in the most amazing and gentle ways. And if you are not sensitive enough to detect His voice you will quench it, and your spiritual life will be impaired. This sense of restraint will always come as a "still small voice" (1 Ki. 19:12), so faint that no one but a saint of God will notice it.[3]

This is a key thing in walking with Him. When I feel that sense of restraint, that "check" in my spirit, I know I need to follow it, even though sometimes I don't know why. Sometimes I discover why later, but even when I don't, I've learned to trust that still, small voice.

How to hear God's voice

How do I hear the voice of God, you may wonder? There are many wonderful books and resources on hearing God's voice, and I will share some of them here. It often is just slowing down, quieting our hearts with the word, and listening.

Be one of His sheep

Jesus tells us we need to be one of His sheep to hear His voice. *"My sheep hear My voice, and I know them, and they follow Me"* (John 10:27). (As mentioned earlier, if you are not sure you belong to Jesus, please check Appendix A for the steps to become one of His followers).

You have probably also heard many stories about how sheep can tell their own shepherd's voice from all the others. That comes from spending time with their Shepherd.

Walk close to God

Jesus also tells us He wants us to *"abide"* in Him (John 15:4). In her "Hearing Jesus" podcast, Rachel Goll says that time in the Word is one of the best ways to hear the voice of Jesus, to be able to tell it apart from other voices.[4] Prayer, worship, and listening for that small, still voice are all part of abiding.

Derek Prince has written a book about hearing God's voice. He says that we hear God's voice in our hearts. He gives the example of a bank where only the manager's voice opens the safe deposit area.[5]

Derek's book *How to Hear the Voice of God* lists six ways to do it. He states we need to cultivate sensitivity to God's voice like the fingers of a blind person are sensitive to Braille.[6] He thoroughly describes six ways to cultivate that sensitivity:

- Attention
- Humility
- Time
- Quietness
- Worship
- Waiting[7]

A preacher named Robert Morris also gives specifics on how to hear God's voice. He produces videos for his TBN show *Frequency*. He lists four steps to hearing God's voice in one of his shows, "How Valuable is Hearing God's Voice to You?"

- Set an appointment, time, and place
- Be still and worship (quiet your mind)
- Pray and read the Word
- Listen and write[8]

What hinders hearing God's voice?

Many things can hinder our hearing the voice of God, but I will mention just a few of them here.

Pride

Derek Prince lists humility as number one on his list of ways to cultivate sensitivity to God's voice. He describes how the humility of confessing sin removes barriers to hearing. James 4:6 says God *"resists the proud, But gives grace to the humble"* and in verse 8 he says: *"Draw near to God, and He will draw near to you."*

I remember the day I wandered in the hills above my house trying to decide if I should leave my husband. I had started the relationship with the woman for whom I eventually left him. I felt strong emotions for her, and my mind was racing, thinking of all the financial and family consequences of divorce.

Instead of spending time in the Word and asking Jesus what to do, I let my emotions decide. I thought life is short, and these feelings were too powerful to ignore. I was listening to the cheetah within, as best-selling author Glennan Doyle describes in *Unchained*. The cheetah wanted what it wanted. I was like one of the children of Israel who *"would not hear, but stiffened their necks, like the necks of their fathers"* (2 Kings 17:14).

There was a hesitation in my spirit, which I now know was from Him, but I chose to ignore it because I wanted what I wanted. I didn't humble myself to hear from God.

Idolatry

Isaiah talks about "dull hearts" and how poor hearing is a result of idolatry, which *"make the heart of this people dull, And their ears heavy, and shut their eyes; lest they see with their eyes, and hear with their ears, and understand with their heart, And return and be healed"* (Is. 6:10).

Idolatry made my hearing dull at times. Even as I've walked with Jesus, codependency or overattachment can make me prone to not listening to His small still voice. When I think about someone too much, I know it's time to ask His forgiveness and turn my heart and ears to Him.

Pain

Pain can also be a barrier to hearing the voice of God. It's easy to become bitter and question God in times of pain or when God seems silent.

Pain can also lead some people to open their hearts and seek God if they haven't listened to Him. Mark Batterson quotes C.S. Lewis: "God whispers to us in our pleasures but shouts in our pain."[9]

Jesus tells us to expect times of pain and testing in this life, but we may find them confusing. He tells us not to be surprised by these times and to prepare our hearts for them. (Note the section in Chapter 8 on hardships and testing for more discussion of this.)

The Psalmist encourages us to make these places of pain a spring of water. *"Blessed is the man whose strength is in You, Whose heart is set on pilgrimage. As they pass through the Valley of Baca [weeping], They make it a spring . . . They go from strength to strength"* (Ps. 84:5–7).

Peter told us about the positive results of suffering when he stated, *"But may the God of all grace, who called us to His eternal glory by Christ Jesus, after you have suffered a while, perfect, establish, strengthen, and settle you"* (1 Pet. 5:10).

How to confirm God's voice

It is essential to hear God's voice correctly, and Derek Prince has outlined some ways to confirm it. He says you should ensure the following:

- Agreement with scripture (which includes rejecting counterfeits)
- Circumstances lining up
- Peace in our heart[10]

Of course, agreement with scripture is the most important, but the third item, seeking peace in my heart, has also been key in making decisions, one my mother always brought up when I had to make a difficult real estate decision.

Everyone in my family advised me one way except my mother. She said to pray about it and seek God's peace. I wasn't comfortable doing what the other family members recommended and did not have peace about it. I followed my mother's advice. There were a few setbacks initially, but time has shown it to be a great decision.

Learning to hear God's voice will be key in your walk with Him and help you stay close to Him. *"He who has ears to hear, let him hear!"* (Matt. 13:9).

Your Shepherd knows you by name. He wants to be close to you, and He wants you to hear His voice.

I Need More . . .

About Hearing God's Voice

- *Hear God's Voice,*
  by Derek Prince

- *Whisper:*
  How to Hear the Voice of God,
  by Mark Batterson

10

Following Jesus

My finger was literally on the button. Everything in me wanted me to click Like and Share. Why am I not doing it? I thought. The author of the meme was a Christian, the quote sounded positive and life-affirming, and it would certainly encourage and uplift my social media friends. I still can't do it. But why? With my index finger lightly tapping on the top of the computer mouse, I sat pondering my hesitation. Then in a sudden burst of clarity, the Holy Spirit was all like, "Snap out of it!" Oh, yeah. I was hesitating because although this quote sounded nice, it was not Biblical. It was actually a lie . . . a happy little lie.

~Alisa Childers, *Live Your Truth and Other Lies*

This quote from the first paragraph of Alisa Childers's book demonstrates her sensitivity to the Holy Spirit and obedience to Him.

He will give you "stop" signals

Looking back over the years, I have learned that Jesus often gives me stop signals. They are subtle and easy to miss, but when I listen for that "still small voice," I know from experience when it is Him.

Oswald Chambers describes this process well in *My Utmost for His Highest*:

> But then as we grow spiritually, we live so fully aware of God that we do not even need to ask what His will is because the thought of choosing another way will never occur to us. If we are saved and sanctified, God guides us by our everyday choices. And if we are about to choose what He does not want, He will give us a sense of doubt or restraint, which we must heed. Whenever there is doubt stop at once. Never try to reason it out, saying, "I wonder why I shouldn't do this?" God instructs us in what we choose; that is, He actually guides our common sense. And when we yield to His teachings and guidance, we no longer hinder His Spirit by continually asking "Now Lord, what is Your will?[1]

This a good description of these little "stop" signals. I have found that these are especially important to listen to when distancing myself from a codependent relationship. Often, like for Alisa, it's related to social media posts: keeping a low profile and not posting anything at all unless I feel He wants me to. I have found social media can just prolong a connection that needs to be weakened.

As mentioned in Chapter 3, one of Lori Thorkelson's guidelines is to "begin gradually separating yourself from your partner." She goes into great detail and gives the example of a man named John who resisted it. His dependent partner began attending a different Bible study—and he found "a very good reason" to switch to the same one. He also felt the Holy Spirit nudging him to get rid of certain record albums or tapes (the ones containing "our song"), but he kept forgetting to do it.[2]

I have learned that the sooner I follow the Spirit's gentle directions, the sooner the issue is resolved. Sometimes for me it has meant staying away from a Bible study like in the example above.

I love what Lori says later in her booklet. "The immediate reward of giving up a dependent relationship is peace with God. Even amid pain over the loss of dependency, we experience peace, relief, and joy as our fellowship with God is restored. 'It's like waking up after a bad dream,' one woman told me."[3]

Yes, I have found that to be true.

He will give you "go" signals

Another part of obedience is to obey "go" signals. Psalm 23:2b says of the Good Shepherd, *"He leads me beside the still waters."* Sometimes, the waters seem turbulent, but when I let Him guide me, He takes me to a place of calmness and rest. Psalms also reminds us that *"He leads me in the paths of righteousness for His name's sake"* (Ps. 23:3).

Scripture tells us repeatedly that God wants us to follow His commandments. It gets a little trickier when we want to know what to do in specific situations. There are many examples in Scripture of people not knowing what to do and going to God to ask Him. We are told that this pleased Him.

King David was one example of a person who often asked God what to do. The next scriptures are examples of times when David did this got an answer, and obeyed what the Lord asked him to do.

> *So David inquired of the Lord, saying, "Shall I go up against the Philistines? Will you deliver them into My hand?' And the Lord said to David, 'Go up.'"*
>
> 2 Sam. 5:19

> *Now there was a famine in the days of David for three years, year after year, and David inquired of the Lord. And the Lord answered ... So they performed all that the king commanded. And after that, God heeded the prayer for the land.*
>
> 2 Sam. 21:1,14

We know God was pleased with David because he was called a man after God's own heart (1 Sam. 13:14).

Barriers to Obedience

Many things can be barriers to obedience, but I will mention just two: questioning and heart trouble.

Questioning

Jonah is a good example of someone who questioned God. He didn't want to go to Nineveh because it didn't make sense to him.

The Assyrians were enemies known for being evil. Jonah couldn't understand why God loved them and would allow them to repent. He tried to run away but eventually went to Nineveh and preached to the people. After the people repented, the Lord told him:

> *And should not I pity Nineveh, that great city, in which are more than one hundred twenty thousand person who cannot discern between their right hand and their left?"*
>
> Jonah 4:11

God had a reason for His direction and wanted Jonah to obey, whether he understood or not.

I mentioned earlier that a couple of long-term friendships got confusing. In one of them, we didn't see each other very often but when we did, she would hug me several times with eyes glowing and tell me how much she loved me. I know it was innocent on her part but for me it sent off alarm bells.

I was caught off guard because there had never been a hint of anything inappropriate, but I knew I needed to distance myself from the friendship. It was easy for me to fall into a "poor me" attitude and question why this beautiful friendship would have to be put on hold until it returned to a normal range of feelings.

The words from Ecclesiastes 3:5 echoed in my head: *"a time to embrace, And a time to refrain from embracing."* This was one friend I knew I needed to refrain from embracing.

Not fair! I thought. Many people tell me they love me and give me hugs and I have many long-term friendships of twenty-five to thirty years with no problems. Plus, I'm a hugger and enjoy hugs from everyone, so why not from someone I care deeply about?

But I knew I had to follow His instruction to *"keep your heart with all diligence"* (Prov. 4:23) and not let the friendship slip into codependency. I had questions but knew I had to be obedient.

Heart Trouble

The Bible often mentions hard hearts and stubborn hearts. It tells us in Hebrews about the children of Israel hardening their hearts:

> *Therefore, as the Holy Spirit says: "Today, if you will hear His voice, do not harden your hearts as in the rebellion, in the day of trial in the wilderness, where your fathers tested Me, tried Me, and saw My works forty years."*
>
> Heb. 3:7–9

In my life, a hard heart caused me to leave my husband. It started with small areas of disobedience. If I'd been listening to Jesus, I never would have visited that "gay church" at all. I had the excuse in my mind that I wanted to interview gay people and persisted in attending even after I knew an attraction had started. I knew it was wrong but ignored His voice and moved forward.

As I continued to disobey, my heart got so hard I stopped caring about listening or following the Lord but just wanted to do what I wanted.

Psalm 81:11–12 sums up what happened to me quite well:

> *"But My people would not heed My voice . . . So I gave them over to their own stubborn heart, To walk in their own counsels."*

Benefits of Obedience

The Bible lists many benefits to obeying Him. I have found that the closer I follow Him, the more benefits I experience. Here are some He has promised us:

- He will give you the Holy Spirit. "*And we are His witnesses to these things, and so also is the Holy Spirit whom God has given to those who obey Him*" (Acts 5:32).

- He will purify your soul. "*As obedient children, not conforming yourselves to the former lusts, as in your ignorance . . . since you have purified your souls in obeying the truth through the Spirit in sincere love of the brethren, love one another fervently with a pure heart*" (1 Pet. 1:14, 22).

- He will give you peace. "*Oh, that you had heeded My commandments! Then your peace would have been like a river, And your righteousness like the waves of the sea*" (Is. 48:18).

  "*My son, do not forget my law, but let your heart keep my commands; for length of days and long life and peace they will add to you*" (Prov. 3:1-2).
  "*Great peace have those who love Your law*" (Ps. 119:165).

- He will be with you. "*Paul was compelled by the Spirit, and testified to the Jews that Jesus is the Christ. . . . Now the Lord spoke to Paul by night in a vision. 'Do not be afraid, but speak, and do not keep silent. For I am with you, and no one will attack you to hurt you, for I have many people in this city'*" (Acts 18:5,9-10).

- He will love you and manifest Himself to you. "*He who has My commandments and keeps them, it is he who loves Me. And he who loves Me will be loved by My Father and I will love him and manifest Myself to him*" (John 14:21).

- He will be honored. "*If you abide in Me, and My words abide in you, you will ask what you desire, and it shall be done for you. By this My Father is glorified, that you bear much fruit."* (John 15:7–8).

- **He will give you joy, and you can rest in His love.** *"If you keep My commandments, you will abide in My love, just as I have kept My Father's commandments and abide in His love. These things I have spoken to you, that My joy may remain in you, and that your joy may be full"* (John 15:10–11).

- **He will know that you love Him.** *"He who has My commandments and keeps them, it is he who loves Me"* (John 14:21).

Aren't these wonderful promises? I have experienced these in my life, and I wouldn't trade them for anything. That's not to say there haven't been hard times, but what could ever compete with these beautiful gifts from God?

Your Good Shepherd will lead you beside still waters and to green pastures, places of peace and joy. He wants you to follow Him.

11

Wholehearted Living

"We're a team for Jesus," Molly would often say. Molly and I were "sidekicks" in our small church for several years. She was the church "grandma," and people would come to her for cough drops or a Kleenex, but mainly for a big smile from her heart. She often said to me and others, "I love you with the love of the Lord." And we knew she meant it.

One of my earliest memories of Molly was when I visited her and watched her give a few dollars to a young church leader. She asked him to put them under the phone book in the church kitchen for a refugee family to pick up so they could buy rice. She would also purchase bus tickets and leave them in the church office for people who might need them.

Molly created a beautiful flower arrangement for the church altar from her garden every Sunday. She loved flowers and her face would light up every time she was able to give a rose or some mint from her garden to people who visited her home.

Molly's eyes sparkled and she always had a big smile when she talked to people. She mentioned Jesus in almost every conversation with strangers or other believers. Her smile got even brighter when she raised her hands and sang during church worship. She often said, "We're a team for Jesus," while pointing her index finger skyward.

Molly never gossiped or criticized anyone but would say, "That was different," if someone did something wrong. When she passed away, people at her memorial service people spoke of Molly's joy and how she shared it with everyone she met.

I still smile when I think of Molly. She loved Jesus and others with her whole heart.

He wants you to have an undivided heart

Scriptures tell us that God is searching for *"those whose heart is completely His"* (2 Chron. 16:9 AMP). His Word makes it clear that we can't hide our hearts from Him. *"For the Lord does not see as man sees, for man looks at the outward appearance, but the Lord looks at the heart"* (1 Sam. 16:7).

I've found that it's easy to love and serve Him over time while part of my heart is devoted to something else. My heart is easily divided. I can look great on the outside, but the inside needs attention.

Some kings who ruled Israel gave examples of a divided heart and how God views that. In 1 Kings 12:28, Jeroboam set up some high places with golden calves at Bethel and Dan, which were illegal places to worship Yahweh.[1] He made shrines in the high places that *"he had devised in his own heart"* (1 Kings 12:33).

The two kings who reigned after Jeroboam did the same thing. They did everything right in the sight of the Lord, except they continued with these places of worship that were not God-ordained. Amaziah was one example.

> *And he did what was right in the sight of the Lord, yet not like his father David . . . However the high places were not taken away, and the people still sacrificed and burned incense on the high places.*
>
> 2 Kings 14:3, 4

These kings lost their kingdoms. God let them know He was upset about what they did and wanted them to follow Him wholeheartedly as David did (2 Kings 14:8).

Different forms of idolatry divide the heart

Idolatry is a big heart divider and can take many forms besides same-sex attractions. Dr. Michael Brown defines it thus: "Idolatry is when we take the trust or adoration that belongs only to God and give it to anyone or anything else."[2]

It says in Jonah 2:8 NLT that those who worship false gods *"turn their back on all God's mercies."* Christians can make even good things like Christian service an idol because there is so much positive feedback. Looking back, I can see times when I enjoyed serving but left God out.

Oswald Chambers describes this problem well:

> Are you obsessed by something? You will probably say, "No, by nothing," but all of us are obsessed by something—usually by ourselves, or if we are Christians, by our own experience of the Christian life. But the psalmist says that we are to be obsessed by God. The abiding awareness of the Christian life is to be God Himself, not just thoughts about Him.... A child's awareness is so absorbed in his mother that although he is not consciously thinking of her, when a problem arises, the abiding relationship is that with the mother. In that same way, we are to "live and move and have our being" in God (Acts 17:28) . . . To be obsessed by God is to have an effective barricade against all the assaults of the enemy.[3]

So, what do we do about this human tendency? It often means an "attitude adjustment" of checking in with Him, asking for and listening to His directions. Becoming aware of these things is an excellent first step to dealing with them. Then we can eliminate them. As General Boykin said, "Rid yourself of whatever separates you from God."[4]

People-pleasing divides the heart

People-pleasing is like the idol of Christian service, and I find it easy to slip into. I can do things to help one particular person, to lighten their load. For me, this has shown up in going beyond what's expected to see someone's smile.

This happened at times when I felt like everything depended on me for a particular ministry, and I would fill in every missing gap. I felt responsible for ensuring everything happened perfectly, no matter how much time and effort it required.

These are ministries that I believe in, and I admire the people leading them, but I forget to ask God if it's what He wants me to do. At some point, I realize I'm serving a person or people rather than the Lord.

He specifically asks us not to be men-pleasers in Ephesians 6:6–7, *"Not with eye service, as men-pleasers, but as bondservants of Christ, doing the will of God from the heart, with goodwill doing service, as to the Lord, and not to men."* Paul calls us out when we do things to look good to others.

My Utmost for His Highest leads off with the scripture, *"We make it our aim . . . to be well pleasing to Him"* (2 Cor. 5:9). Oswald Chambers says:

> It requires a conscious decision and effort. . . . It means holding ourselves to the highest priority year in and year out; not making our first priority to win souls, or to establish churches, or to have revivals, but seeking only to be "well pleasing to Him."

Then Chambers further says:

> At least once a week, measure yourself before God to see if your life is measuring up to the standard He has for you. Paul was like a musician who gives no thought to audience approval, if he can only catch a look of approval from his Conductor.[5]

I once heard a good suggestion for those prone to pleasing people: "If you want to practice not being a man-pleaser, do something that only God will know about."

Woundedness divides the heart

Over the years, I have found that the Lord has revealed areas of wounding in my heart that have needed healing and pointed to a need to forgive myself and others. A wounded heart is a restricted heart, hindered from being entirely devoted to Him.

When my father was dying a few years ago, I helped my mother take care of him, and later, when my mother was dying, my sister and I took care of her. Over the years, and especially during those later years, I learned more about myself and my parents, which gave me a better understanding of all of us.

My relationship with my father was never emotionally close, but in his later years, I wanted it to be. I was helping my mom take care of him, and each night, when I left to go home, he would sit in his recliner by the door. I would kiss him on the forehead and say, "I love you, Dad." He always said, "We love all our children," until just before he died, when he finally answered, "I love you too."

During those years, I learned more about what he suffered in childhood. His mother died giving birth to him, and he was shifted from relative to relative as he grew up. I never realized how much some of these things affected him until, in his last weeks of life, he shared with a caregiver his feelings of guilt for his mother dying because of him.

Something else I learned about him caused me to think his heart had softened toward same-sex-attracted people. He had performed a funeral for a black man who died of HIV AIDS when no one else would. He had never discussed this; I only learned about it after discovering the cards and gifts the grateful family had sent him.

I also learned some new things from my mom in her last days. She told me that when I was two, and my sister was born, she started spanking me every day because I kept climbing up to look into my sister's crib. That probably happens to many kids, but I have no memory of it and was surprised to hear it.

I began to wonder if all those spankings shocked my little system. My mom told me I was the center of attention as the first and only child before my sister arrived. Could this have been part of a root of a need for same-sex affirmation? It's hard to say, but it did make me aware that many things happen to us as children we have no way of knowing unless someone tells us.

While writing this book, I met with a counselor a few times to process some things that came up. It wasn't fun to revisit all of it, but seeing her helped a lot. We discussed many things, including these stories about my parents and other issues. She shocked me one day when she suggested I pray to forgive my mother. I thought I had forgiven my mom but realized I hadn't prayed about it very much. The process peeled another layer off the onion and opened areas for healing.

I Need More . . .

Support for Family and Friends

- "Hope Group for Family and Friends" PortlandFellowship.com
- Restored Hope Network: restoredhopenetwork.org

Guilt also resurfaced as I reflected on my life and thought about how my decision to leave my husband affected my children and grandchildren. They are doing well, but some are not believers, and I know that deep inside, they carry some scars from my choices.

Over the years I have met Christian parents who are heartbroken over their children's struggles with LGBT issues. It has been touching to hear the parents share the depth of their confusion and heartbreak over their children's choices. It feels so personal to think of how much I hurt my parents and that they had to keep it to themselves in those days. There were no support groups for them, and discussing such things in the church was taboo.[6] This has caused more profound love and compassion for them and a chance to ask the Lord to forgive me for hurting them so much.

The bottom line is that all these realizations have provided opportunities for the Lord to restore wounded areas of my heart through forgiving myself and others—areas where others hurt me and I had hurt others.

Psalm 147:3 tells us, *"He heals the brokenhearted, And binds up their wounds."*

He wants you to examine your heart

Christopher Yuan summarizes some of our heart problems in his book *Out of a Far Country: A Gay Son's Journey to God. A Broken Mother's Search for Hope*. He advises us to look at our hearts and ask:

> What do I think I can't live without? This was the question I had been asking and finally, I was finding some answers, I was realizing there were a lot of things I could live without—and it was very freeing. I was not controlled by my past addictions, my old idols, my sexual attractions, or my sexuality. What do I think I can't live without? Well, there was one thing, or more specifically one person, I knew I couldn't live without—Jesus. And I needed more and more of Him each day.[7]

I've learned that it helps to periodically do a heart check-up and ask the Lord if I follow Him wholeheartedly. *"Search me, O God, and know my heart, try me, and know my thoughts"* (Ps. 139:23 KJV). And Proverbs 4:23, *"Keep your heart with all diligence, For out of it spring the issues of life."* Some things I discover in heart check-ups shock me, but becoming aware helps me get back on track.

I'm sure your life experiences are different, but as you look back through your life, it is good to bring it before the Lord and ask Him to show you if any areas of hurt need to be healed. Ask Him to show you if there is anyone you need to forgive, including yourself. He wants your heart to be whole and undivided. *"Unite my heart to fear your name"* (Ps. 86:11).

He wants to give you a rejoicing heart

When I allow the Lord to show me any divided areas of my heart and seek His forgiveness, the joy is great.

Jesus summarizes all the commandments to be to *"love the LORD your God with all your heart"* (Matt. 22:37). One of the benefits of loving Him with our whole heart is that He will give us a rejoicing heart like Molly had.

Samuel reminded the people to *"serve Him in truth with all your heart, for consider what great things He has done for you"* (1 Sam. 12:24). David gives us an example of praising God with his whole heart: *"I will praise You, O LORD, with my whole heart, I will tell of all Your marvelous works"* (Ps. 9:1).

I pray that you will know the joy of serving God with your whole heart and quickly know when it starts to stray so you can get it back on track. You will be blessed! As it says in Psalm 119:2: *"Blessed are those who keep His testimonies, Who seek Him with the whole heart!"* I pray that you can learn to love Jesus and others as Molly did with your whole heart!

Your Good Shepherd wants your whole heart, and He will give you a rejoicing heart.

Part IV

Looking Ahead

12

Entering the Promised Land

What does it mean to come home? People talk about entering the Promised Land as coming home, or as the endpoint; maybe you've heard that too. The promised land is portrayed as a beautiful place to arrive after wandering in the wilderness. It felt like I was coming home and entering the promised land when I gave my heart to Jesus.

But the scriptures tell us the children of Israel still had battles to fight and enemies to overcome in the promised land. It wasn't their final destination of peace and safety.

Nor does Jesus promise that following Him will mean the end of our battles in this life. We continue on our journey, whether in the wilderness or the promised land, and will always have challenges to overcome and battles to face. But we do look ahead to our final destination.

In the meantime, the Bible gives us great examples and instructions for coping with any difficulties we may face. For example, Moses gave some instructions to the children of Israel as they entered the promised land, and they provide good reminders for us as we journey on.

When Moses gave the people a plan of action for surviving and thriving in the promised land, he told them to be prepared to fight, not to be afraid, and that the Lord would fight for them (Deuteronomy 11 and 12). Some of his instructions are as follows.

Preparing To Go In

Moses' first command to the people was to go in.

> *Look, the* LORD *your God has set the land before you; go up and possess it.*
>
> Deut. 1:21

Don't be afraid

Moses encouraged them, "*Do not be terrified, or afraid of them. The* LORD *your God, who goes before you, He will fight for you, according to all He did for you in Egypt before your eyes, and in the wilderness where you saw how the* LORD *your God carried you, as a man carries his son, in all the way that you went until you came to this place*" (Deut. 1:29–31).

Moses reminded them of all that God had done for them to bring them through the wilderness.

Entering In

As the people entered the land, Moses gave them instructions that have been repeated throughout Scripture in various ways. Let's look at the instructions Moses gave.

Keep the commandments

Moses told them five times to keep the commandments. (Deut. 11:1; 8, 13, 22; 12:28). Three of these times, he said the greatest commandment was to love the Lord God and serve Him with all the heart and soul (Deut. 11:1, 13, 22).

Moses told them in these verses the benefits they would have if they kept the commandments:

- They will be strong and possess the land (11:8)
- They will have rain (11:13)

- They will dispossess greater and mightier nations than themselves because the Lord will drive out their enemies (11:22)
- The Lord will enlarge their borders (12:20)
- It will be well with them and their children forever (12:28)

Don't do what is right in your own eyes

It is our default position to do what we think is right. Moses reminds the people, *"You shall not at all do as we are doing here today—every man doing whatever is right in his own eyes"* (Deut. 12:8), because this will keep them from the rest and inheritance the Lord was giving them including *"rest from all your enemies round about, so that you dwell in safety"* (12:10). They were promised rest from their enemies and to live safely if they refrained from doing what was right in their own eyes.

Don't be deceived

> *Take heed to yourselves, lest your heart be deceived, and you turn aside and serve other gods and worship them.*
>
> Deut. 11:16

It's that deception and idol worship again. These are common traps for same-sex-attracted people and for most humans. It's so important that we not let our hearts be deceived or get into idol worship.

Remember His words

> *"Lay up these words of mine in your heart and in your soul . . . You shall teach them to your children, speaking of them when you sit in your house, when you walk by the way, when you lie down, and when you rise up.*
>
> Deut. 11:18–19

Moses reminded them to remember his words, which are now part of the Word of God. He told them of their importance and instructed them to pass them on to their children.

Have a rejoicing heart

Moses instructed the children of Israel three times to worship and bring their sacrifices to God *"with rejoicing"* (Deut. 12:7, 12, 18). Moses gave us an example of this as recorded in the song of Moses. *"I will sing to the LORD, for He has triumphed gloriously . . . The LORD is my strength and my song, And He has become my salvation. He is my God and I will praise Him; My father's God, and I will exalt Him"* (Exod. 15:1–2).

Then Moses continued for the following eighteen verses in praise and worship, thanking God for the many ways He had taken care of the children of Israel in the wilderness.

God wants us to have a rejoicing heart. It puts the focus on Him.

Let Him fight for you

Later in Deuteronomy, Moses reminds the people that when they go into battle, it's the Lord who fights for them.

> *"Do not be afraid of them: for the LORD your God is with you, who brought you up from the land of Egypt. . . . Do not let your heart faint, do not be afraid, and do not tremble or be terrified because of them; for the LORD your God is He who goes with you, to fight for you against your enemies, to save you."*
>
> Deut. 20:1b, 3b–4

In the scriptures, we are reminded over and over again to let Him fight for us. It's so easy to try to do things independently and forget to ask for His help, but we miss out on His power when we do that.

Remember God's attributes

Moses also reminded the people of the attributes of God. *"He is your praise, and He is your God, who has done for you these great and awesome things which your eyes have seen"* (Deut. 10:21). He constantly reminded them that "it's all about Him."

Summary of Instructions

Reading these instructions, I can see their application to our spiritual battles and our walk with Him. Here is a summary of these points of Moses, and six other points from this book.

- Keep the commandments
- Don't do what is right in your own eyes
- Don't be deceived
- Remember His words
- Have a rejoicing heart
- Let Him fight for you
- Remember God's attributes
- Don't be afraid
- Walk closely with Him
- Cry out to Him when you are in trouble
- Inquire of Him about what you should do or not do
- Follow what He tells you to do
- Give Him the credit for the victory

These key points from scripture have made all the difference in my journey, and I know they will also make a difference for you.

Benefits of Entering In

What does all this boil down to? We may have some hard times walking with Jesus, but there are also many benefits.

If I could speak to my younger self thirty-five years ago in Portland Fellowship, I would tell myself it will be worth it to follow Jesus. When I look at the peace and joy He's given me as

I've walked with Him, my loss of the fear of death, and the many wonderful life experiences He has brought to me, I don't regret a minute of it.

In his video "The Slow Death of Marriage," Becket Cook mentioned being aware of his gay women friends being scarred by multiple relationships.[1] I know that would have happened to me if I had continued in gay relationships. Like he said elsewhere, each new boyfriend he thought would be "the one," and I've heard women say the same thing—the perfect one to meet my needs is just around the corner.

In the church I attended with my former partner, we often attended "holy unions," which was what was provided for gay couples before marriages were legal. My partner and I never had one because we noticed that when the ladies had a holy union, they would break up shortly afterward.

Most of our female friends lived together for five to seven years and tended to live in serially monogamous relationships. The love seemed to meet those deep needs for a while, but after time, it didn't. I wish I could tell them that Jesus can fill that void.

My biggest regret in life is that I entered that gay relationship. I often wish I could have a "do-over" and stay in my marriage, or if we separated, to live by the scriptures. I know Jesus has forgiven me, but there is a lingering sadness over what my life could have been like, especially for my children, if I hadn't taken that course of action.

I encourage you, dear reader, to follow Jesus in chastity and according to Biblical guidelines. If you are in a same-sex relationship or tempted to enter one, I urge you to get out and stay out. It may seem tempting and irresistible, but I know you will want out at some point and wish you hadn't made that choice.

I've shared the benefits I've enjoyed over the years of following Jesus, and He also offers those to you. He has given His Word with guidelines to live by and instructions to help us cope with difficulties. The best part of the whole deal is that we have the promise of a future home where there will be no more sadness, sorrow, or tears. And our Good Shepherd will bring us there.

As far as benefits, I've listed some of the benefits of obedience in Chapter 10 and in the first part of this chapter. Let me review a few of the benefits we can enjoy now and what we have to look forward to in our future forever home. Some have been mentioned before and others have not.

Benefits for Now

Peace	*Thus says the Lord, your Redeemer, the Holy One of Israel: I am the Lord your God, who teaches you to profit, who leads you by the way you should go. Oh, that you had heeded My commandments! Then your peace would have been like a river, and your righteousness like the waves of the sea (Is. 48:17–18).*
Strength of Soul	*I will praise You with my whole heart . . . in the day when I cried out, You answered me, and made me bold with strength in my soul (Psalm 138:1-3).*
Joy	*You will show me the path of life; in Your presence is fullness of joy (Ps. 16:11).*
Blessings	*Blessed are the undefiled in the way, who walk in the law of the Lord! Blessed are those who keep His testimonies who seek Him with the whole heart (Ps. 119:1-2).*
Abundance	*The Lord is my shepherd (to feed, to guide, and to shield me), I shall not want (Ps. 23:1 AMP).*
A Full Life	*The Good Shepherd says: "I came that they might have life, and have it in*

abundance (to the full, till it overflows)"
(John 10:10 AMP).

Benefits for the Future

Eternal life and security	*My sheep hear My voice, and I know them, and they follow Me. And I give them eternal life, and they shall never perish; neither shall anyone snatch the out of My hand (John 10:27–28).*
Rewards	*And when the chief Shepherd appears, you will receive the crown of glory that does not fade away (1 Pet. 5:4).*
No More Tears or Death	*And God will wipe away every tear from their eyes; there shall be no more death nor sorrow, nor crying. There shall be no more pain, for the former things have passed away. Then He who sat on the throne said, "Behold I make all things new" (Rev. 21:4,5).*

The apostle Paul tells us Jesus *"abolished death"* (2 Tim. 1:10). Not only is the fear of death gone, but death itself! Of course, that doesn't mean we won't die, but our best life will begin when our physical body dies. He has promised us eternal life with Him.

The other day, I read a verse that made my heart happy. I hadn't noticed before that all the animals, even sea creatures, will be around the throne of God in heaven, joining in praise and worship. Can you imagine that? This scene is so beautifully described in Revelation:

Then I looked, and I heard the voice of many angels around the throne, the living creatures, and the elders; and the number of them was ten thousand times ten thousand, and thousands of thousands, saying with a loud voice: "Worthy is the Lamb who was slain to receive power and riches and wisdom, And strength and honor and glory and blessing!" And every creature which is in heaven and on the earth and under the earth and such as are in the sea, and all that are in them, I heard saying: "Blessing and honor and glory and power be to Him who sits on the throne, And to the Lamb, forever and ever!

Rev. 5:11–13

This gives an image of the Lamb who died for us, and the fact that He is also our shepherd is pictured clearly in Revelation 7:14b–17. This passage refers to those who have come out of the great tribulation and gives us a beautiful image of our Good Shepherd and His heart for us.

So he said to me, "These are the ones who come out of the great tribulation, and washed their robes and made them white in the blood of the Lamb. Therefore, they are before the throne of God, and serve Him day and night in His temple. And He who sits on the throne will dwell among them. They shall neither hunger anymore nor thirst anymore; the sun shall not strike them, nor any heat; for the Lamb who is in the midst of the throne will shepherd them and lead them to living fountains of waters. And God will wipe away every tear from their eyes."

Rev. 7:14b–17

Our Shepherd will lead us to springs of living water. That bears repeating! *"For the Lamb who is in the midst of the throne will shepherd them and lead them to living fountains of waters. And God will wipe away every tear from their eyes."* It doesn't get any better than that!

I hope this book has been helpful and encouraging to you and that you will keep it as a reference to remind yourself of the promises of God when times are tough or you have doubts. His Word is a reliable guide for your best life now and your forever life at home with Him. You will have the best of both worlds.

Your Good Shepherd will take good care of you in this life, and then after you die, He will bring you to your eternal home with Him.

> *Oh come, let us worship and bow down;*
> *Let us kneel before the* L*ORD* *our Maker.*
> *For He is our God,*
> *And we are the people of His pasture*
> *And the sheep of His hand.*
>
> Psalm 95:6–7

Appendix A

Steps to Becoming a Follower of Jesus

Joel Rosenberg of the Rosenberg Report[1] gave a wonderful testimony the other day about how his parents had become believers and took him to church, and he wasn't too happy about it. He went to sword drills and memorized scripture and learned to do all the things expected of him in Sunday School, but his heart wasn't in it.

Then as a teenager, he went through a dark place. He even thought of writing a book about suicide. He was in his room on his bed and really "having it out" with God. "Where are you?" he asked. "Do you exist? Why don't I know you?"

Then he heard God whisper in his heart, "Have you ever read my Word to learn about Me? Have you ever talked to Me, just like you would to a friend?"

That brought Joel up short. He realized he hadn't and began to do so. It was a pivotal moment in his life, and after that, he began to sense God's presence and realness in his life as he put God's Word into practice.

Joel chose to believe in God and became a true follower of Jesus Christ. You can make that choice as well. The information below developed by Pastor JD Farag of Calvary Chapel, Kaneohe,[2] explains how you can do that:

ABC's of Salvation

The gospel is God's good news to us:

> *I declare to you the gospel which I preached to you . . . that Christ died for our sins according to the Scriptures, and that He was buried, and that He rose again the third day according to the Scriptures.*
>
> 1 Cor. 15:1–4

Admit that you're a sinner. This is where that godly sorrow leads to genuine repentance for sinning against the righteous God and there is a change of heart, we change our mind and God changes our hearts and regenerates us from the inside out.

Believe in your heart that Jesus Christ died for your sins, was buried and that God raised Jesus from the dead. This means trusting with all your heart that Jesus Christ is who he said he was.

Call upon the name of the Lord. *"For whoever calls upon the name of the Lord shall be saved."* Romans 10:1

These are step-by-step instructions to become a follower of Jesus. **Don't wait; do it right now—He is so worth it!**

Visit ChatAboutJesus.com or RealAnswersToLife.com, or call or text Need Him Ministries at 888-537-8820 if you need to talk to someone.

It's important to tell someone of your decision and to find a good church where you can get to know other believers and grow in your new relationship with Jesus.

Welcome to His family!

And then, why not share the good news with a friend?

End Notes

Introduction
[1] Jeremy Howard (general editor), *Holman Study Bible*, NKJV (Nashville, Tennessee: Holman Bible Publishers, 2015), 1386.

Chapter 1 – Living My Truth
[1] Beckett Cook, *Change of Affection: A Gay Man's Incredible Story of Redemption* (Nashville Tennessee: Nelson Books, 2019), 2, 72.

[2] Christopher Yuan and Angela Yuan, *Out of a Far Country: A Gay Son's Journey to God, A Broken Mother's Search for Hope* (New York: Waterbrook Press, 2011), 11.

[3] Rosaria Champagne Butterfield, *The Secret Thoughts of an Unlikely Convert: An English Professor's Journey into the Christian Faith* (Pittsburgh, PA: Crown and Covenant Publications, 2014), 2.

Chapter 2 – It's about Love, Isn't It?
[1] Anne Witton, "The Lesbian Urge to Merge" Same-Sex Attraction (blog) livingout.org, February 2023.

[2] Al-Anon FamilyGroups, The Twelve Steps, Step 11, al-anon.org/for-members/the-legacies/the-twelve-steps

[3] Beckett Cook, "Why Does God Care About Your Sex Life?" Beckett Cook Show, episode 48, YouTube, becketcook.com.

[4] Ron Mehl, *The Tender Commandments* (Sisters, Oregon: Multnomah Publishers. Inc, 1998), book cover.

[5] Cook, "Why Does God Care?"

[6] Sheila Walsh interview, TBN, Matt and Laurie Crouch, March 21, 2023.

Chapter 4 – Healing Your Heart
[1] Witton, "The Lesbian Urge to Merge"

[2] Debra Fileta, *Reset* (Eugene, Oregon: Harvest House Publishers, 2023), 13, 14.

³ Anne Paulk, *Restoring Sexual Identity: Hope for Women Who Struggle with Same Sex Attraction* (Eugene, Oregon: Harvest House Publishers, 2003), 69, 70.

⁴ Paulk, *Restoring Sexual Identity*, 52.

⁵ Gina Ryder, "Attachment Trauma: Effects, Examples, and How to Heal," Psych Central, Jan 19, 2022 ("What Is Attachment Trauma?" psychcenter.com/health/attachment-trauma).

⁶ Carolyn Pele and Philip Sutton, "Sexual Attraction Fluidity and Well-Being in Men: A Therapeutic Outcome Study," Journal of Human Sexuality, Volume 12, Summer 2021, 61–86.

⁷ Robert Weiss, "Lesbian Women, Love Addiction, and the Urge to Merge," An Interview with Dr. Lauren Castine, Psych Central, Dec 10, 2015 (psychcentral.com/blog/sex/2015/12/lesbian-women-love-addiction-and-the-urge-to-merge-an-interview-with-dr-lauren-costine).

Chapter 5 – Feeding You Well

¹ Tara-Leigh Cobble, "The Bible Recap," thebiblerecap.com/start.

² Bible Study Fellowship, bsfinternational.org

³ Brian D'onofrio and Robert Emery, "Parental Divorce or Separation and Children's Mental Health" (Pub Med Central, World Psychiatry 2019, February 18).

Chapter 6 – Support If You Fall

¹ Dave Carder, *Anatomy of An Affair: How Affairs, Attractions, and Addictions Develop, and How to Guard against Them* (Chicago, Illinois: Moody Publishers, 2008, 2017), 75.

² Christopher Yuan, *Holy Sexuality and the Gospel: Sex, Desire, and Relationships Shaped by God's Grand Story* (Penguin Random House, New York: Crown Publishing Group, 2018), 44.

Dr. Yuan holds to a Biblical sexual ethic but takes a different approach than those in redemptive healing ministries such as Restored Hope and Portland Fellowship.

³ Lori Thorkelson Rentzel, *Emotional Dependency and How to Keep Your Friendships Healthy* (Downer's Grove, Illinois: Intervarsity Press, 1990), 8.

⁴ Rosaria Champagne Butterfield, *Openness Unhindered: Further Thoughts of an Unlikely Convert on Sexual Identity and Union with Christ* (Pittsburgh, Pennsylvania: Crown & Covenant Publications, 2020), 86.

⁵ Rentzel, *Emotional Dependency*, 9.

⁶ Rentzel, *Emotional Dependency*, 9, 10.

[7] Rentzel, *Emotional Dependency*, 12-16.

[8] Rentzel, *Emotional Dependency*, 28.

[9] Rentzel, *Emotional Dependency*, 28.

[10] June Hunt, "Hope for the Heart," hopeforthe heart.org.

[11] Focus on the Family, focusonthefamily.com.

[12] Restored Hope Network, restoredhopenetwork.org.

[13] Neil Anderson, *The Steps to Freedom in Christ Study Guide: A Step-by-Step Guide to Help You* (Minneapolis Minnesota: Bethany House, 2014) (Now published by Baker House).

Chapter 7 – Dealing with Opposition

[1] Jeremy Howard (general editor), *Holman Study Bible, NKJV* (Nashville, Tennessee: Holman Bible Publishers, 2015), 746.

Chapter 8 – Evading Deception, Traps, and Detours

[1] Christopher Yuan and Angela Yuan, *Out of a Far Country: A Gay Son's Journey to God, A Broken Mother's Search for Hope* (New York: Waterbrook Press, 2011), 185-186.

[2] Beckett Cook, "There is no such thing as a 'Gay Christian' " Beckett Cook Show, episode 58, YouTube https://www.becketcook.com.

[3] John Bevere, *The Bait of Satan: Living Free from the Deadly Trap of Offense* (Lake Mary, Florida: Charisma House, 1994, 2011), 18.

[4] Charles Spurgeon, "Discernment Spurgeon Quote" girdedwithtruth.org, October 9, 2009.

[5] Alisa Childers, *Live Your Truth and Other Lies: Exposing Popular Deceptions That Make Us Anxious, Exhausted and Self-Obsessed* (Carol Stream Illinois: Tyndale House Publishers, 2022), 4.

[6] Childers, *Live Your Truth*, 66-67.

[7] Bevere, *Bait of Satan*, 6.

[8] Andrew Brunson, "Fear God, Not People," June 1, 2022, decisionmagazine.com/fear-god-not-people.

[9] Andrew Brunson, "Prepare to Stand," YouTube, Evangelical Presbyterian Church, June 19, 2022.

Chapter 9 – Walk Closely with Jesus

[1] Mark Batterson, *Whisper: How to Hear the Voice of God* (Colorado Springs: Multnomah Random House, 2011), 10.

² Batterson, *Whisper*, 9, 10.

³ Oswald Chambers, *My Utmost for His Highest*, Oswald Chambers Publications (Grand Rapids, Michigan: Discovery House Publishers, 1992), August 13.

⁴ Rachel Goll, "Hearing Jesus" podcast, shehears.org.

⁵ Derek Prince, *How to Hear God's Voice* (New Kensington, PA: Whitaker House, 2020), 76, 77.

Derek Prince was a beloved Bible teacher who passed away a few years ago, but his work is still available at Amazon and teaching tapes on YouTube.

⁶ Prince, *How to Hear God's Voice*, 79.

⁷ Prince, *How to Hear God's Voice*, 93.

⁸ Robert Morris "How Valuable is Hearing God's Voice to You?" from his show on TBN "Frequency," August 29, 2021, watch.tbn.org/robert-morris-frequency.

⁹ Batterson, *Whisper*, 172.

¹⁰ Prince, *How to Hear God's Voice*, 130.

Chapter 10 – Following Jesus

¹ Oswald Chambers, *My Utmost for His Highest*, Oswald Chambers Publications (Grand Rapids, Michigan: Discovery House Publishers, 1992), June 3.

² Lori Thorkelson Rentzel, *Emotional Dependency and How to Keep Your Friendships Healthy* (Downer's Grove, Illinois: Intervarsity Press, 1990), 28–30.

³ Rentzel, *Emotional Dependency*, 35.

Chapter 11 – Wholehearted Living

¹ Jeremy Howard (general editor), *Holman Study Bible, NKJV* (Nashville, Tennessee: Holman Bible Publishers, 2015), 569.

² Dr. Michael Brown, Instagram, 11/6/22 @drmichaelbrown.

³ Oswald Chambers, *My Utmost for His Highest*, Oswald Chambers Publications (Grand Rapids, Michigan: Discovery House Publishers, 1992), June 2.

⁴ Guest Speaker: LtGen. William G. Boykin, World Outreach Church, June 26, 2022.

⁵ Chambers, *My Utmost for His Highest*, March 17.

[6] Portland Fellowship offers a support group for parents, family, and friends of those with LGBT issues. It is called the Hope Group and is available in person and via Zoom and includes people from all over the country. Also, Restored Hope has connections with similar groups in various areas of the USA.

[7] Christopher Yuan and Angela Yuan, *Out of a Far Country: A Gay Son's Journey to God, A Broken Mother's Search for Hope* (New York: Waterbrook Press, 2011), 189.

Chapter 12 – Entering the Promised Land

[1] Beckett Cook, "The Slow Death of Marriage," Beckett Cook Show, Ep. 104, January 5, 2023.

Appendix A

[1] Joel Rosenberg, "The Rosenberg Report." Trinity Broadcasting Network, Saturday, November 26, 2022.

[2] JD Faraq, "The ABC's of Salvation," Calvary Chapel Kaneohe, office@calvarychapelKaneohe.com.